LAW STU~ ~~ ~~~ ~~~~~ ~ ~

OF

TRIAL & ERROR: Volume One

• "The book is amazing! It definitely was a page turner... The book showed the realities of being a lawyer and the effects it can have on your life, physically and emotionally.... It was a great eye-opener into the complicated world of criminal law... I can't wait for a sequel!"

• "TRIAL & ERROR has re-ignited my passion for law... Every story taught me something about criminal law. I would recommend this book to anyone considering or enrolled in law school. The book is an exceptional account of the battles won and lost in the world of freedom lawyering and the pursuit of justice."

• "TRIAL & ERROR is very insightful not only to criminal law but to the world of legal practice and life. Each case captured an important lesson of being an attorney... The book is an interesting, honest insight into the criminal law that I've never experienced before... It has given me a much more realistic idea of what the field of criminal law is out in the real world.

• "The book provides comical relief and hope for someone with the aspiration of one day achieving success as a trial lawyer... From the moment I picked up this book I was immediately rejuvenated."

• "TRIAL & ERROR has shown me that rapport with clients and people in general makes an outstanding lawyer... It also highlights mistakes made by the budding defense attorney and what was learned from them... I too struggle with public speaking and eloquence. Reading of the author's struggle inspired me... The cases exemplify what is essential to becoming a successful trial lawyer."

TRIAL & ERROR
The Education of a Freedom Lawyer
Volume One: For the Defense
Arthur W. Campbell

LAW STUDENT REVIEWS
OF
TRIAL & ERROR: Volume Two

• "Excitement, frustration, worry, compassion, awareness, suspense, confidence, amusement, and surprise are only a few examples of the feelings I experienced during Campbell's rollercoaster of a journey. Each story is written so intelligently; [together] they provide a fun and easy read. Campbell's raw honesty and wit make his books relatable. They will provoke the reader's thoughts and feelings."

• "This book [was] even more exciting to read than the first. It was interesting to compare and contrast Mr. Campbell's experiences on both sides of litigation. This was especially apparent in his internal battle between "freedom lawyer" who wanted justice for those who had no power, and "warrior" who would stop at nothing to win. I think the combination of the two mindsets contributed to his success in prosecuting those he thought were truly guilty, while still protecting their liberties by not taking every low blow possible."

• "I cannot even describe how many life lessons were in this book! I could see that even brilliant professors were once where I am now, as a beginner in the chosen profession. They learn too, every day, literally through trial and error. I think this is not the last time I read the book. It will serve me as a great guide to being a good lawyer."

• "These stories were inspiring in that they showed me both what I aspire to be, a lawyer who is brave enough to practice freedom law, as well as what I aspire not to be, a lawyer who apathetically or cowardly falls short of her responsibility. Further, these stories showed me the importance of competence, professionalism, and humility. [Finally, these episodes] highlighted the intellectual challenge and how important it is to be able to "think on your feet" at a criminal trial."

TRIAL & ERROR
The Education of a Freedom Lawyer
Volume Two: For the Prosecution
Arthur W. Campbell

PROFESSIONAL & STUDENT REVIEWS
OF
TRIAL & ERROR: Volume Three

• "Through Campbell's stories of wit and irony, I relived many of my own courtroom battles. In this third volume Campbell completes a life-long search to integrate freedom law with his sense of self by confronting his warrior face-to-face. Actually his relentless pursuit of awareness and self-honesty is an exemplar for all of us who search for purpose and integrity in our lives. Both humbling and inspiring, the trilogy of TRIAL AND ERROR is a must-read for all law students and freedom lawyers— and especially for those facing the cross-roads of a career."
—Nancy Song, veteran Public Defender

• "Buckle up — you can't learn this stuff in a law book! At the turn of every page I discovered something that would otherwise take me years of my own trials and errors to understand. More than just courtroom stories, this book makes you reflect on your own life's journey. Thanks to Campbell we can all become better students of life. I want my own [life] to contain as much insight and vigor as he has for practicing and teaching freedom law."
—Ashley Turner, law student

• "Inspiring! Everyone who seeks truth, justice, and the vindication of the innocent will enjoy and benefit from Campbell's collection of glorious vignettes. The author's brutally truthful accounts shine light on the human factor inside the criminal courtroom and provide valuable guidance to lawyers courageous enough to practice freedom law in the labyrinth of our criminal justice system."
—Professor Laurence Benner, a former Chief Public Defender and member of the Board of Directors of the National Legal Aid & Defender Association

TRIAL & ERROR
The Education of a Freedom Lawyer
Volume Three: Return to the Defense
Arthur W. Campbell

TRIAL & ERROR

The Education
of a
Freedom Lawyer

VolumeThree:
Return to the Defense

by
Arthur W. Campbell

Poetic Matrix Press

ISBN: 978-0-9852883-3-4

Poetic Matrix Press
www.poeticmatrix.com

You protect the rights of many
when you defend the rights of one.
—Judge Norbert Ehrenfreund

How do we transform mere power into justice?
—Barack Obama

A person who is tired of crime is tired of life.
—John Mortimer

CONTENTS

This volume is dedicated
to one of the nation's premier clinical programs:
D.C. Law Students in Court

FOREWORD

by Charles A. Bird

Mr. Bird was lead appellate partner at Luce, Forward, Hamilton & Scripps, LLP in San Diego, California and has served in many volunteer roles including president of the ACLU of San Diego and Imperial Counties, and a director of Federal Defenders of San Diego, Inc. and Appellate Defenders, Inc., also of San Diego.

Art Campbell writes a good story. That's reason enough to read this book. But there's more.

This is a book for lawyers of any age who wonder what to do with their tools and careers. That's pretty much all of us attorneys, at least some of the time. It is also a book for anyone who aspires to be a lawyer or wants to know what a first-class lawyer does and thinks.

Good stories enable us to live briefly in the experience of the characters. In Art's stories, we experience representing people who are unconventional, whether by poverty, personality or principle. By respecting the rights of these challenging people, the Constitution and international law restrain power's insistence on submission.

Whatever philosophers or theologians may say of the source of liberty, pragmatically it flows from the rule of law. Order and liberty, an inseparable duality, push and pull daily in courts high and low. Preventing too much order from stifling liberty is the special business of the freedom lawyer.

Personal messages also flow from Art's stories. For me, two predominate.

First, every lawyer should be a freedom lawyer, at least some of the time. It feeds the soul in a way that transcends professional achievement and feeding one's family. Using the tools for the sake of the good probably would save many lawyers from spirals of burnout and addiction sadly common in our profession.

Not every freedom lawyer must go to court, as Art's teaching career shows. Indeed, Art and I met as members of a board that guides two indigent criminal defense organizations. Opportunities for transactional lawyers abound.

Second is the evolution of the warrior. Art's stories show us that those who aspire to excellence as freedom lawyers must cultivate four iconic characters: storyteller, warrior, scholar and sage. Of the warrior, Art mostly portrays the young fighter. In my experience, the mature warrior is a character of discipline and perseverance.

At argument in my own favorite freedom-lawyer case, my warrior kept his flowing emotions secret as a justice of the California Supreme Court savaged my opponent. Then warrior laser-focused his own rebuttal and closed with time on the table. Think of this evolution again as you read Art's epilogue.

Now let Art's stories enlighten.

INTRODUCTION

Who and what are freedom lawyers? They come in every size, age, and gender. They practice in all fields of law. They work in every section of the globe and quarter of society. They aim to foster human freedom and oppose injustice.

Two prior volumes in this trilogy depicted me in roles most people see as polar opposites: first, criminal defense attorney and then as prosecutor. In each role I pulled a different end of rope our adversary system uses in its tug-of-war. Yet that rope of justice stayed the same.

Each episode revealed different challenges as I confronted forces, both external and internal, that stood between my clients and my view of justice in their case.

My first book's trials introduced me to the depth and breadth of justice in a court of law— surprises, flukes, and defects intermixed with pragmatism, truth, and politics.

The second volume recognized a potent comrade in the courtroom. Beside my freedom lawyer stalked a warrior who would fight for victory at all costs. Once those costs meant I convicted someone who was innocent— and the price I paid to set him free.

Not until the middle of the current volume did I discover what my warrior fed upon. That resolved much turmoil in my life— as a lawyer and a man— and led to probing deeper towards my core.

Blowing dust from private trial notes helped me draft the first two books. But when I reached this volume's murder case I'd ceased keeping notes. Nonetheless some clients of that time still stamp down hallways of my mind; now they mingle in a single chapter: "Further Freedom-Law Adventures."

As before, and out of similar regard for peoples' privacy, these pages often cloak their characters with pseudonyms and fictionalized peripherals.

This book brings readers through my final years in Washington, D.C., touches on my life in academia, and concludes with People versus Drusilla Campbell et alia. At that time it was the largest mass-protest trial in San Diego history. It was the last and most important trial of my career. Yes, the lead defendant was my wife.

The Education of a Freedom Lawyer

Volume Three:
Return to the Defense

WHAT, PROCURING SEX AGAIN?

There's nothing better in the world than hearing "not"
in front of the word "guilty." — Unknown source

Spring hailed my drive along Virginia's parkway by raising
tiny fists of chartreuse leaves. I'd recently resigned my post
as Special Assistant U.S. Attorney for Washington, D.C. Now
I was returning to that city and my former role defending
those accused of crime.

I parked, brushed my brief-less case against my thigh,
and climbed the granite stairs where once I'd labored
as a prosecutor. But this time I walked inside the lawyers'
entrance to an office of the courthouse clerk.

On his counter lay a chipped clipboard where attorneys
registered to represent the city's recently arrested indigents.
On the list, which later swelled to fifty-seven names, mine
was seventeenth.

An hour later I returned, blinking twice at the defendant's
name the clerk had matched to mine: Manstead Armstrong.
As prosecutor I'd convicted him some months ago of
attempting to procure for prostitution purposes.

Freedom lawyer shook his head: *Just after his release from
jail, he gets busted for the same offense!*

An elevator dropped me to the courthouse lockup where
I met the virgin client of my new career. Manstead's
wardrobe hadn't changed: torn shirt, trouser stains, and
filthy canvas shoes.

His face was patched with islands of a scruffy beard. As
I approached, he raised two fingers to his face and formed
a cross: "No, Campbell, you can't be for the defense!"

"Manstead, it's your lucky day. Shows Lady Justice has a
sense of humor…"

"… or she's really into irony," Armstrong added with a grin.

3

I rolled up my appointment document and thrust it through the latticed bars. "You don't have to take me as your lawyer. Shall I ask the judge to get you someone else?"

"Hell, no!" he said. "I'm glad to have you on my side this time."

I told Manstead that the day I had convicted him I'd sent a memo to my fellow prosecutors, warning them about the power of the "con-man defense" he had raised. Someone charged with attempt-pimping might claim he'd simply tried to trick his victim out of cash, not broker fees for prostitutes.

To stymie this, I'd urged an easy fix: When prosecutors saw a case like this, they should "charge 'in the alternative' attempted false pretense."

But my memo had been knocked aside by juggernauts of mass-production justice clanking down the courthouse halls. Today that oversight would clear the way for our defense. A second plus would be my plan that Manstead demonstrate his con-man hocus pocus to a jury of his peers, not just talk about it to a hardened trial judge.

At that time I didn't realize the outcome of our case would rest upon a gambler's bet: Can planned pluses outweigh unexpected minuses dropped on the other side of Blindfold Lady's scales?

Armstrong's prior record kept him bail-less in jail until trial. But I made sure when he appeared before our jury he was showered, shaved, and dressed in decent clothes.

On trial day our first minus dropped from courthouse skies: Judge Norma Johnson was assigned to try our case. "Well, Mr. Campbell, I see you've moved back to defense." Although she wrapped her greeting in a tone of cordiality, her glare suggested she had not forgotten the rape case I had once defended in her court.

Not only had I bickered with her rulings, I'd provoked the prosecutor into paroxysms of machismo. Like the school marm she had been before her law career, Judge Johnson had to scold us like two wayward playground kids.

Minutes later the next minus leapt into this case. During voir dire of our juror candidates I asked the routine question: "Have any of you had encounters with the law?" A young woman stood and scowled at me.

I inquired, "Would you prefer to answer at the bench where it's more private?"

The woman raised her chin another inch above her blue-tweed suit and said, "No, Mr. Campbell, that's not it. I feel you're talking down to us. You needn't treat us in this way."

To my alarm, other jurors nodded their accord. I tried to hide the gulp beneath my tented brows of genuine concern. Freedom lawyer flashed an instant replay of voir dire, trying to perceive my queries from a juror's point of view:

We're near the end of month-long service, suffering through platoons of lawyers trying to impress us with superior smarts. Courtroom questions have been repetitious, boring, glib, and asked like we've not heard them scores of times.

Abruptly warrior spied my paradox: *What the hell can you do now? You're trapped inside an igloo of resentment— but breaking out could bury you inside a blizzard of hostility.*

I chose to freeze in place and ask the standard follow-up: "Ma'am, would your reaction to my questions influence your ability to render a fair and impartial verdict in this case?"

"No, sir," she sighed, staring at her shoes while shaking her head slowly back and forth.

I approached the bench and asked Judge Johnson to excuse the entire panel, as all jurors were now poisoned toward defendant's side. She said, "Mr. Campbell, I'm afraid that's too drastic a solution to a problem— if there is one— that you've caused all by yourself."

Silently I ground my teeth and requested she at least exclude this candidate for cause. Judge Johnson smiled broadly and replied, "Your motion is denied."

I was forced to utilize one of my few peremptory challenges (ones for which no reason need be given) to remove Ms. Bluesuit from our panel.

But her outspoken honesty and my fear that it would taint our jury made me stumble: I used two more peremptories to banish juror candidates I'd earlier decided would be good for our side of the case.

Warrior jabbed me in the ribs: *Calm down, Art! You've been forced to ante for what seemed your snooty stance toward jurors. Now don't throw away your other chips!*

During prosecution's evidence, my learned opposition played his cards the way I had a few months earlier: He called a plain-clothes officer as his first witness. The square-jawed man told how he had approached my client and inquired, "Hey, where's the action in this town?"

Armstrong had allegedly replied, "I'll put you with some girls who'll drive you wild— but first you've got to show me you've got cash." The officer asked what services he'd get. When Armstrong listed sundry sex acts and their price, the cop arrested him.

On cross-exam I didn't try to smear the cop's veracity or smudge his version of the street-side dialogue. I just enlarged the scene so it was set for our defense.

Q. Officer Bramwaddle, before you placed my client in your car, you searched him, right?

A. Yes, sir, we did.

Q. And you found two envelopes inside his jacket, didn't you?

A. Yes, that's right.

Q. One envelope was empty and the other stuffed with paper, cut the size of dollar bills?

A. Yes, sir, that's also true.

"No further questions for this witness," I declared and took my seat.

A second vice-squad officer testified he'd seen his partner and my client from across the street. The prosecutor needed this corroboration of the incident. Again my turn arrived to cross-exam.

Q. Detective Thrubworth, isn't it a fact that from where you stood you could see the sidewalk on both sides for an entire block?

A. Yes, sir.

Q. And at the time you watched your partner and my client have their talk you didn't see even one unescorted woman on the block, did you?

Q. No, sir, can't say that I did.

"Thank you— that's all," I said and once more took my seat.

The prosecutor smiled and announced, "Your honor, ladies and gentlemen of the jury, the government now rests." I made a routine motion for dismissal, expecting it would be denied. Judge Johnson didn't thwart my prophecy.

I turned to the jury, quickly scanned their faces, and said, "The defense calls the defendant, Manstead Armstrong." My client, one-hundred pounds packed on a skeleton of five-feet-four, rose like he was starring in a documentary.

Warrior warned: *Watch out— he's a brassy con-man, jumping at the chance to sell twelve jurors his best scam!*

Manstead marched across the courtroom, trying to upgrade his normal slinky gait by tilting back his head and thrusting out his chest. He wore a light-green zipper jacket and new running shoes, compliments of counsel for defense. Regrettably the pants and shirt I'd purchased were too large; they draped his boney frame like sheets around a starved cadaver.

Armstrong's testimony opened with a bang— the same way it had before. Facing toward the jury box, he said, "Everything those vice-squad officers said to you was true— except I wasn't selling sex. I'm just a penny-ante con man."

Five jurors leaned forward so they wouldn't miss what he'd say next: "My whole game is lifting dough from guys in search of sex. But the officer arrested me before I finished my routine. What I always tell the mark is that my fee is fifty bucks and he's got to show he's got the cash."

As planned, at this point I stopped Armstrong. "Let's pretend that I'm your mark," I said, pulling out my wallet, then extracting two twenties and a ten.

Armstrong slid a slender hand inside his jacket, drawing out an empty envelope. He said, "I tell the man 'I'll seal your money in this for safe-keeping'." Armstrong slipped my bills inside his envelope, licked its glue-strip seal, and tucked it in an inner-pocket of his coat.

He went on, "Sometimes this makes the guy suspicious. If so, I tell him he can hold the envelope himself and hand it to the girl he'll meet on the next block. If the guy says 'Yes,' I reach back in my jacket."

As jurors strained to watch, Armstrong pulled an envelope from his coat and handed it to me. "Looks and feels like the same envelope," I said.

"Counselor, you can't testify!" boomed Judge Johnson.

"I apologize, your honor. I got caught up in the con."

"That's *enough,*" the judge admonished. "Are you finished with your witness, Mr. Campbell"

"Almost, your honor. Mr. Armstrong will you show the jury what's inside this envelope?"

Manstead took it from me, tore it open, letting bill-sized papers flutter to his lap. "I just switch the stash," he said, taking out and tearing open the first envelope. He fanned the bills and gave them back to me. "By the time the guy discovers there's no girl and opens up his envelope, I'm long gone."

"No further questions," I announced. As I passed by the prosecution desk I saw my former colleague's eyebrows jump at one another like mad caterpillars. On behalf of my unheeded memo, I tossed him a wink.

But now our case collided with a third surprising minus. Armstrong, stage-struck by his own performance, turned arrogant on cross-exam. At first his casual responses implied the prosecutor's questions about where, when, who, and how were too dim-witted to be taken seriously.

Then Manstead tried to twist each answer back to his con-man defense. "Well, Mr. Lawyer for the government, if you'd have been there you'd be fooled just like other marks I've conned."

Norma Johnson cast a frown from her judicial throne: "Mr. Armstrong, you must answer counsel's questions straight-away. This is a court of law, not some corner on 10th Avenue."

"I'll keep that in mind," was Armstrong's near-contemptuous response. I winced, watching shock or grimaces appear on every juror's face. I caught Manstead's glance, fired back a somber look, and shook my head.

He got my message but the harm was done. Warrior muttered, *Manstead, your attitude's as welcome as a blast of hippo gas— and most jurors won't acquit defendants they don't like.*

When Armstrong's cross-examination ended, Johnson banged her gavel on the bench. "Court will *recess* for today." My grade-school heart leapt at that word and tugged my sleeve. But warrior's arm just felt fatigue: *It only took ten minutes for our client to destroy the case we'd built for him!*

Driving home I watched fog slide across the parkway on slick snail feet. Tomorrow our defense would need some other plus to counteract the jury bias Armstrong— and his counsel— had let glide into this trial.

Warrior summed things up: *We've only got a dark horse in this race, so it needs to surge the final stretch. Your argument had better spur it home.*

Forty minutes later my Camaro crunched through gravel at our cottage in Virginia's countryside. By that time freedom lawyer had decided we would stack imagined cinder blocks before the jury box.

I'd suggest to jurors if they sat atop this wall and overlooked their biases, they'd see the prosecutor's case was just a leaky boat awash inside a sea of doubt. Drusilla helped me reinforce this metaphor, rehearsing me far past our suppertime.

Next day with an unassuming voice I began to build our wall. I started with some added facts that had surfaced during trial. Armstrong's bust was Thrubworth's first arrest; he'd only worked two days in vice. In case he had to play a drunk, he'd consumed a shot of scotch "or maybe even two."

I reminded jurors that this backup cop had stayed across the street and candidly confessed he hadn't heard a single word my client spoke. "Yet he filled out and signed the arrest report, studded with verbatim quotes from Mr. Armstrong."

Piling on more blocks, I said, "That same officer admitted he'd not seen my client with a lady of the night, nor were there any women without escorts as far up and down the block as he could see."

Building towards a rampart, I reviewed my client's courtroom demonstration: "Wasn't that believable, so convincing it was almost chilling, don't you think? But also think on this: That night if Mr. Armstrong *had* flim-flammed some playboy's cash, wouldn't that sex-hungry guy receive what he deserved?"

For the keystone of our wall, I requested Manstead stand and face the jury box. "Ladies and gentlemen, look at this man's size. Do you believe there's any way that he could make it as a brawny street-pimp on 10th Avenue?"

I stepped back, urging jurors to scrutinize the evidence from atop our wall. "The prosecutor's boat is leaky to begin with; think of all those holes appearing in its hull. But his fatal flaw was launching the wrong boat. He didn't charge my client with the proper crime."

Shifting weight, I went on: "Sure, Mr. Armstrong's guilty of attempted false-pretenses. He truthfully confessed this crime to you. But he's charged with attempting to *procure* for *prostitution* purposes."

I thanked the jury and sat down. Freedom lawyer wondered, *Will our jurors lay aside their prejudice against a haughty lawyer and his brash conceited client? Will they step up to my rampart's view and see the prosecution's sinking craft?*

Judge Johnson gave instructions on all elements of attempting to procure, plus rules of reasonable doubt. Jurors ambled in a line from their paneled box, coalescing into clusters as they exited the room. In an hour they came back.

After all these years I still feel a frisson up my spine,
recalling how it felt to stand with an accused, turn to
face twelve jurors, and await my client's fate.

This time "Not guilty" was their call.

All right! warrior cheered inside my chest. *Great Caesar's
ghost,* said freedom lawyer, *it feels great to be back on
defense's side!*

That afternoon I sped home on the parkway just ahead of
rush-hour cars. The sun splashed paint on roadside rocks.
After mentally replaying highlights of the trial, I scrolled
through a list of restaurants where I'd dine tonight with
Timeless Bride.   We'd celebrate our mutual victory; her
coaching made the odds reverse their tipping point.

Racing past the budding sycamores, I yelled, "Told you so!"
to former colleagues on the prosecution's side. If they'd
not overlooked my memo, there'd have been no trial;
Manstead would have pled to attempted false pretenses.
What almost trounced me months ago when I'd prosecuted
Armstrong had transformed to our winning strategy.

STREET JUSTICE OVER COURTROOM LAW

Justice... that fugitive from the camp of conquerors.
— Simon Weil

A brisk spring afternoon greeted Burl Everwood when he parked his Cadillac coupé on 7th Street, D.C. Burl and three friends exited the car and strolled along the sidewalk, heading for Fast Eddy's Carryout.

They didn't get ten yards before a foot-beat cop accosted them. "License and registration, please," said Joshua Hardtemple, smiling, holding out his empty palm.

"I don't have to show you any goddamn *driver's* license I'm *walking!* Are you blind?"

A flurry of harangues ensued between the officer and Burl, his senior by three decades. Their insistence and resistance quickly drew a crowd.

Bystanders backed Everwood, tossing fusillades of curses under First Amendment flags. To them it was another case of cop harassment of the city's common folk. Hardtemple snatched a walkie-talkie from his belt and barked a code for back-up cops.

Moments later a shiny Black Maria screeched against the curb; four officers jumped out. Everwood's prior passengers quickly blended with the crowd but Burl stood his ground.

When he again refused to show his papers, two cops grabbed him, shackled both his wrists in steel cuffs, and packed him in their van. Four ill-fated dominoes began toppling down Burl's corridor of life.

First Hardtemple emptied Burl's pockets. He found the Caddy's registration, listing Everwood as owner. But the driver's license actually belonged to someone else. Now the cop could lodge a charge of "driving on another's license," more serious than not carrying his own.

Using Burl's keys, the officer unlocked the coupé and climbed inside the car so he could drive it to the city's impound lot. That's when he saw the butt end of a pistol leaning toward him from an arm-rest in between the two front seats.

Checking records at his precinct, Hardtemple found out neither pistol nor its ammo had been registered and Burl had no license to possess a firearm. Thus fell three more dominoes.

Next day the arraignment judge assigned me to defend Burl on four charges: Driving on Another's License; Possession of Unregistered Firearm; Possession of Unregistered Ammunition; and, the most serious, Carrying a Pistol Without a License.

An hour before Burl was arraigned I interviewed him in the courthouse lockup. I made four phone calls from the lawyer's lounge to verify the bail information he'd supplied.

Burl was a skilled bricklayer with three years of ties to his community. These, I later argued to his honor, justified my client's bail on personal recognizance. The judge agreed and Burl was freed.

Everwood assured me he and his three passengers would drop by my office next week to work out a trial strategy and rehearse their testimony. Meanwhile I dispatched Ron Rogers— a volunteer from George Washington School of Law to dig out copies of police reports.

If my scholar gum-shoe found discrepancies between police accounts and Burl's version of the facts, he'd drive to the scene and try to track down witnesses. If cops had shaded statements from what actually occurred, we'd need impeachment testimony.

But Ron found no major discord in the various accounts. More troubling was the fact that neither Burl nor his passengers showed up at my office. *Damnit!* freedom lawyer said. *I got him out on bail. Wasn't that enough to show he hasn't got some flunky Fifth Street lawyer— that I take his troubles seriously?*

Besides this slap at freedom lawyer's pride, warrior didn't want to lose a case from lack of witness preparation. He grumbled, *Burl and his buddies stood up for their rights on 7th Street. Now why won't they haul their butts a few blocks to my office, so we can mount a good defense?*

I'd bumped into this position during days of student lawyering. Some clients fought for civil rights and dignity in squabbles on the street, then seemed gripped by the futility of doing so inside a court.

Reminding warrior of those days, freedom lawyer chided, *Hey, try a little empathy! Why should poor folks trust in legal systems seen as hammers for the rich, always banging them like helpless nails?*

But warrior brightened up when freedom lawyer added, We won't need our client's help for one defense. We'll file a pretrial motion challenging the constitutionality of his arrest. Where was Hardtemple's legal cause to halt Burl in the first place? If the cop can't justify that stop, everything he later seized must be suppressed as fruit knocked from a *poisoned tree*.

It's ironic in a freedom-touting country that motions brought to vindicate the Constitution make law-and-order people gag: "Just another slime-ball lawyer trying to divert attention from his client's guilt."

These critics fail to realize our courts perform *two* vital tasks for our republic, not just deciding which of us is guilty of a crime. The judicial branch must also function in our three-boughed government to say if twigs bent by the other two are still constitutional.

Indeed, as happened in this case, when cops arrest someone without a warrant their actions are *presumed* unconstitutional. This means police must prove in court there were "exigent circumstances," facts that would have justified a warrant and no time to find a judge.

So my motion meant the prosecution had to cough up evidence to validate Burl's stop. I sent my client word about our pending hearing, hoping he and fellow travelers would show for what might be their dress-rehearsal for a later trial.

To make an office visit easier, I urged a meeting one hour prior to the hearing. Burl said they all would come but once more no one showed. Instead he and two passengers sashayed into court just as the clerk announced our case.

My learned opposition, Hamilton Turnover, marched to his desk bedecked in self-assurance and a blue-serge suit. He summoned Officer Hardtemple to the witness chair.

Initially the cop asserted he had merely "spot-checked" Burl, a random (i.e. arbitrary) stop to make sure everything was lawful as my client strolled a public street.

Then Hardtemple's explanation bounded to a different knoll: He'd seen my client park a brand-new Cadillac and wanted proof that Everwood was "licensed" to drive cars in Washington, D.C.

When Turnover finished his direct, I stood to start my cross-exam. But first I raised both brows and stared a moment at our motion's judge.

Through crinkly folds of aging flesh, Frank Lamplighter held my gaze as if to say, *Well, Campbell, what's wrong with what the cop just said?*

The judge seemed deaf to Hardtemple's clanging inconsistencies. *Okay,* warrior mumbled sub-silentio, *he won't hear that double pretext for the roust of someone in the ghetto with a pristine Cadillac. And he won't see realities that operate beneath the surface of propriety.*

Today I wouldn't try to make the cop admit his bust was just a ploy. I'd save that for when I stood before a jury of Burl's peers— if this case came to that— not try to sell it to a law-and-order judge.

As they had so many times, freedom lawyer's molars ground against the irony of this soubriquet: *"Law-and-order" folks consistently deny that "law" includes our nation's Bill of Rights!*

Today my cross-examination simply nailed down the cop's two different reasons for his stop. Later I could pry them up at trial.

It came time for the defense to offer evidence if we desired. Sans rehearsal Burl and his two passengers volunteered. The front-seater nonchalantly paddled to the witness chair as if heading up a creek to bag some frogs; inwardly I cringed at what might jump out of his sack.

Some people freeze inside a witness chair. They're suddenly before an audience and attorneys who can't wait to twist their words. They've labored through the oath's solemnity and spy a court reporter poised to capture every utterance. Is it any wonder many can't recount— with relaxed, convincing specificity— what they saw or heard or did at some fast-moving incident?

Another notion flashed through freedom lawyer's mind: *How often has the Blindfold Lady raised the wrong side of her scales because a witness merely couldn't fill the other side with credible descriptions of what happened on the scene?*

So I was all the more surprised to hear our non-prepped witness give a calm, sequential recall of events, unshaken later by Turnover's cross-exam.

That made me take the risk of calling Burl's other passenger, then Everwood himself, to testify. Both were also lucid and avoided getting snagged on cross-exam. What's more, all three portraits of what happened neatly overlapped.

17

But of course they couldn't penetrate Hardtemple's mind and relight the artifice that blazed inside it on the day of Burl's arrest.

Thus, as soon as Everwood stepped down, Lamplighter banged his gavel and upheld the constitutionality of Burl's bust. That made the license, gun, and ammo admissible as evidence because "seized incident to a valid arrest."

On trial day we drew Judge Fred Bulwaddy from the courthouse lottery. He was affable in his late fifties with a curious reputation: Eased out of his law firm and dubbed a judge because he fancied making friendships more than earning fees.

On the bench his concentration sometimes flagged. He'd forget which party raised— or now resisted— issues being argued in his court.

We started at 9:30 on a humid D.C. morning. "Your honor, before our jury candidates arrive, the defense would like to make an oral motion on the subject of voir dire."

"Of course, Mr. Campbell," said Bulwaddy, all smiles and felicity. Warrior wondered, *Does he recall our conversation last week at cocktails for the bench and bar? "Call me Fred!" he'd beamed above a wobbly rye-old-fashioned. Sometimes on the bench his face glowed from a fabled two-martini lunch.*

"Defense moves this court to order the Assistant U.S. Attorney to supply me with a copy of his list of jurors who have been arrested or convicted of a crime."

"What?!" responded Hamilton Turnover.

The judge's face now flashed deep crimson. "Mr. Campbell, I've never heard such nonsense from a lawyer in my life! I'm embarrassed you would waste my time with such a patently frivolous motion."

"With all respect, your honor, it's anything but frivolous. From my experience in Mr. Turnover's office I know trial counsel for the government carry such a document. They use it to decide what jurors to use peremptory challenges against. But that list should not be kept a secret from defense."

Turnover bubbled with expostulation. "Mr. Campbell worked long enough with us to know that record is the product of the U.S. Attorney's office. It's black-letter law that all work-product must be private— immune from forced disclosure to attorneys on the other side."

Trying to maintain my tone as light but positive, I responded, "On the contrary, your honor, what I want are purely public records of arrests. Sure, the data was assembled by the prosecutor's office, but that's because it's the only side with money to compile them."

Catching hesitation in the judge's face, I ratcheted my argument a notch: "Indeed, as an officer of this court, Mr. Turnover should at least hand *you* a copy, so your honor can determine if potential jurors lie to the court when asked if they have been arrested or convicted of a crime."

"So you raise this motion on *my* behalf?" asked Bulwaddy, struggling to align our arguments and frame them in a picture that made sense to him.

"Not just for the court, your honor. The defendant needs a copy as a matter of due process, to make the trial fair for both sides at the bar. My motion's also based on equal protection for an indigent— which court records say my client is. He's wrongly disadvantaged when he can't afford to screen potential jurors with a records check."

Bulwaddy dropped his chin into his hand and stared out the window. Freedom lawyer asked himself, *Which point pierced the palisade that shields this kind man from everything that's unconventional?*

"Your motion's mighty far-fetched, counselor. But I'll err on caution's side where constitutional rights may be concerned. I'll excuse Mr. Turnover for ten minutes so he can make two photocopies of the document, one for the court and one for the defense."

* * * * *

Turnover returned, still flushed with indignation, and handed over copies of his would-be-secret document. In the next hour twenty-four aspiring jurors swore they never had been busted for a crime. But to my delight the prosecutor's dossier disclosed five had records of arrest— two of which had ripened to convictions!

Warrior weighed the choice in front of us: *Should we try to keep those liars on the panel? Odds are they'll be sympathetic to defense. But for that reason Turnover will knock them from the box with his peremptories, jury strikes for which he needn't give a reason.*

Bulwaddy swept away my speculation; he dismissed all five himself. Then he called a side-bar conference to confide to us— and for the record— why he didn't tell these people he'd discharged them for their lies: "Since the prosecutor's records aren't proof-positive those folks were perjurers, such implication from a judge would not be right."

Freedom lawyer smiled: *Always feels good to bend a jurist's resolute devotion to the status quo. How this helps my client, I'm not sure. But if Bulwaddy spreads the word to other judges about prosecutor jury-screens, I've struck a little blow for freedom law. At least in future trials I can cite this case as precedent.*

* * * * *

It was clear Turnover's case would rest on the arresting cop. Keen to bury us, Hardtemple walked calmly to the witness chair and took the oath. He answered questions on direct as if a model of impartiality. If the jury bought his picture of the incident— as did the motions judge— our defense was sunk.

On cross-exam I had to irritate the man, pry up slivers that would prick his arrogance. Jurors needed to perceive that it was he who'd lit the fuse of neighborhood unrest, his prejudice that prompted all the charges in this trial.

Q. Officer Hardtemple, did you decide to stop my client because you didn't like the fact he drove a brand-new Cadillac?

Hardtemple looked surprised but checked his irritation with exaggerated calmness: "No, sir, I didn't care what kind of car he drove."

Q. Well then was it because you didn't like the way my client and his friends walked down the street, ignoring you as if you didn't matter in their world?

The cop clenched his jaw. "No, Mr. Campbell, it was just a routine spot-check."

Q. Didn't you decide to *spot-check* Mr. Everwood because he walked too proud— didn't cringe or shy away— when you yelled "Stop!" and rolled up in his face?

A. I didn't yell. I asked him in a normal tone of voice.

Q. Wasn't it your aim to drop his pride a notch— why else would you demand the *driver's* license for a car he'd parked, from which he'd *walked away?*

Hardtemple's face grew red. "No, sir, what you're saying isn't true! It was just... routine."

Q. Routine for an officer on foot? That day, how many people *walking* down the street did you demand a *drivers'* license from?

A. None, sir, ... but I'd only been on duty for an hour.

Q. Let's be honest, officer, didn't you decide to escalate the situation and arrest my client because he dared talk back to you?

Hardtemple gripped both arms of the witness chair. "Absolutely not! I arrested him because he failed to produce the registration for a car I'd seen him drive."

I gave this response a slight shake of my head, then stepped aggressively toward him, trying to ignite a primitive response.

Q. Isn't it a fact, sir, that you felt you had to bust *someone* for *something* once so many citizens started shouting that you had to call for back-up out of fear for your own safety?

Hardtemple's knuckles turned white gripping both arms of the witness chair, but he couldn't douse the rising decibels and anger in his voice: "No, Mr. Campbell. I just performed my duty as best I could in the circumstances!"

"In circumstances *you* were totally responsible for!"

Turnover leapt out of his chair: "Objection! Campbell's stating a conclusion."

"Sustained," ruled Judge Bulwaddy like an indulgent grandpa.

I took my seat, hoping I'd uncloaked enough of this cop's speedy escalation into rage. Hardtemple hit me with a hostile glare as he stepped down from the witness chair and sculled towards the gallery through his swamp of depthless vanity.

Warrior took stock at this point: *We may have shown a cop's pretext and temper but not Burl's innocence of these four charges. Good thing it's the prosecutor's job to prove he's guilty. And Hamilton will be hard pressed if our jury gets a realistic picture of what happened on that street.*

Turnover put in evidence the other person's driving license, then wrapped up his case by adding three more documents. The latter proved the pistol was unregistered, as was its ammunition, and that Burl had no permit for the gun.

Bulwaddy recessed court for lunch. That gave me ninety minutes to rehearse our defense witnesses: Burl and two passengers.

* * * * *

When the clerk called us to order, Judge Bulwaddy eased himself into his armchair at the bench. *Uh-oh*, warrior warned, *has he just downed another two-martini lunch? On those days his brain returns to court as furry as his words.*

Turnover rose. "May it please the court, if Mr. Campbell plans to call the witnesses he used at the suppression hearing, would your honor ask if they've been warned about their Fifth Amendment rights?"

"Excuse me?" I replied. "The prosecution suddenly desires to safeguard rights for the *defense?*"

I figured Turnover's concerns were purely tactical; he hoped Fifth Amendment fears would scare my people from the witness chair.

"If Mr. Campbell's defense is that Mr. Everwood did not possess the pistol in the car's armrest, then it must have been in the possession of some passenger."

Freedom lawyer cursed himself: *Damn, I've been so focused on the "realistic view," I flew past its consequence! Turnover's right— and I'll get tangled in conflicts of interest if I advise the passengers myself.*

As if glad for time to clear his mind, Bulwaddy recessed court for twenty minutes with instructions to his clerk to snag a couple bodies from the lawyers' lounge.

In due course two Fifth Street attorneys drew aside Burl's travelers for a tête-à-tête. By the time court reconvened and jurors took their seats, both men had declined to testify.

"We'll only call one witness," I told our jury with simulated confidence, "the defendant, Mr. Everwood." Subsequent surprises struck like shin-kicks by a five-year-old who wouldn't stop.

First, I tried to guide my client through the narrative he'd spoken at our hearing to suppress. I tossed standard invitations: "Then what happened?" "And what happened next?" But Burl used each question as a springboard, diving into rants about "the way D.C. police are always ganging up against the poor in our community."

I spent fifteen minutes vainly tossing verbal lassos at my headstrong client, trying to direct him calmly through events from A to Z. Casting glances at the jury box, I saw people look away from him; some stared out the window, some at ceiling patterns, others at the floor.

Eager for a stopping point, after Burl paragraphed his latest diatribe, I pounced: "And that's why you believe you were arrested, Mr. Everwood?"

"Yes," he said, uncrossed his legs, and glared at the arresting officer still roosting in the gallery.

But shin-kicking was not done. During the defendant's cross-exam I sat with mock composure hiding pain as Burl reshaped every prosecution question as he'd done with mine. His egotistic flare-ups made the cop's seem tame.

Warrior muttered, *That's why you always prep a client's testimony! And since you've lost your other witnesses, good luck winning with some razzle-dazzle jury argument. Oh, what the hell, you might as well throw everything you've got.*

When my turn came for final argument, I stood before the jury box and started with a fastball. I wanted it to thump inside the glove of any juror who might need some reason to obey a gut-reaction to this case.

"The prosecution failed its test! It had to prove each element beyond a reasonable doubt. Please, listen to his honor when he points out all the elements the prosecution had to prove. Look how many charges one cop lodged against your fellow citizen, a man who dared stand up to him."

Then I hurled a change-up:"Please don't hold it against Mr. Everwood if he was indignant over his arrest. When he finally got his chance to tell you of the incident, don't blame him that he couldn't stick to simply answering questions. Under our Constitution the defendant doesn't have to testify at all. But my client volunteered because he wanted you to know how strongly he felt wronged."

My notes reflect I spent nearly thirty minutes on my feet, repainting Burl's view, refuting the arresting cop's, reframing the entire incident to one I thought was more consistent with reality. My client was courageous, a man who challenged arbitrary power. By contrast, Hardtemple was a walking law-enforcement hand-grenade without a pin.

Thanks, Cut! warrior thought, remembering my favorite client, a perceptive man who'd urged me to develop empathy.

Next I switched my stance from baseball pitcher to determined carpenter. I jimmied splinters out of what might seem a routine case. My claw hammer wasn't logic; it was hard-edged sentiment.

I asked Burl's peers to look beneath the words of witnesses and documents, to recognize police machismo had provoked the scene. All four charges tumbled from Hardtemple's arrogance followed by attempts to save his face. Jurors first must feel my client's pride, then see how misused police authority had triggered Everwood's self-righteous wrath.

D.C. law kept me from urging that our jury simply overlook my client's crimes. But if jurors felt the load of that injustice on the street, I hoped they'd let it outweigh Burl's minor wrongs.

When I sat down, freedom lawyer was exhausted. But warrior shouted in my ear: *'Sblood, you're back where you belong! You're not just yanking prosecutor levers, dropping bogus charges, urging rehabilitation sentences. You're fighting for street justice from confrontations with a bully dressed in blue— calling on a jury to bring freedom law to D.C. streets!*

In only fifteen minutes jurors trooped back into court. Warrior whispered, *Caution, Art! Twelve people couldn't find a thing to disagree about, even for a quarter-hour. Either they'll hold Burl four times guilty or completely innocent.*

I rose and stood beside my client as we stared across the gulf that separates defendants from their peers. As was their wont, my knees braced to absorb this trial's moment of truth.

Not waiting for the judge to ask, the number-seven juror stood and said she'd been elected fore. Then she sang out loudly, as if speaking for all victims of capricious power, "Mr. Everwood is not guilty on all counts."

Private post-trial notes disclose I stole my strategy from Charlie Foss, one of D.C.'s finest litigators. Last year when I'd been a prosecutor, he'd bested me by arguing twelve jurors should choose justice over strict construction of the law.

Today I'd crafted my own version of this script— with words that came from deep inside my warrior's and my freedom lawyer's bones.

ADDICT AND CONVICT

*At times the law can be a sort of glorified accounting
that serves to regulate the affairs of those who have
power— and all too often seeks to explain, to those who
do not, the ultimate wisdom and justness of their condition.*
— Barack Obama

Jake Maycore had been hooked on heroin. Busted for
possession of his stash, in April he pled guilty when a
prosecutor promised he'd propose probation for a year.

The catch? Jake had to enroll in an experimental rehab
program; every day he must ingest a tab of methadone
dispensed from an official clinic in D.C.

This drug would block his body's need for heroin, thus
help wean him from illegal stuff. But this prescription was
addictive too. So within a week Maycore was hooked again.
Court-required methadone became his body's drug of
choice.

One summer afternoon before a three-day holiday, he
teetered on a cliff of panic: "What if the clinic closes,
stranding me without my daily methadone? I could fall
into delirium tremens, go into convulsions, maybe die."

Maycore might have asked if he could get his weekend
tablet at another clinic. But instead he tucked that
morning's methadone beneath his tongue, pretending
that he'd swallowed it. When the dispensing nurse
glanced away, Jake slipped the pill into the pocket of
his slacks. Today might be a little rough, but at least
he had a tablet in reserve.

That morning Lady Luck, a cousin of Dame Justice, guided
Jake's probation officer to the warehouse where Jake's job
was wrangling flats of foodstuffs with a fork-lift truck.

"Just wondered how you're doing," the official chirped.

But as the officer drew near he said, "Whoa! You're looking mighty sweaty in this air-conditioned place, plus your eyes are red. Better climb down from that cab and let me check you out."

"I'll talk to you from here," protested Jake. "You're not laying hands on me!" The official shrugged, "Have it your way, Maycore," and stamped out the warehouse door.

Ten minutes later two narcotics cops arrived, flashing badges from their wallets. They ordered Jake down from his cab and found his tab of methadone. They cuffed him, took him to their precinct, charged him with possessing an illegal drug.

"But I got it from a D.C. clinic," Jake protested. "You guys hooked me on the stuff!"

"That's why you had to *swallow* it," said one narc. "No problem to possess it in your system, just not on the outside, still in tablet form."

Next day the court assigned me to defend Jake Maycore. Our meeting in the courthouse lockup didn't go down well. I smiled and introduced myself, reaching through the bars to shake his hand.

He backed off, scowled, and shouted, "You're just another trainman for the government that's railroading me to jail!"

I withdrew my hand. "Fine, if that's the way you feel. I've got some other work to do, then I'll come back. Meantime ask around about my rep. If you still feel that way when I return, I'll get a judge to give you someone else."

Thirty minutes later he'd calmed down: "I guess you'll do," he muttered. My first act was bailing Maycore out of jail on his own recognizance.

Next I filed a motion to suppress the tab as seized unconstitutionally. I argued lack of legal cause for cops to bust this man at work. Sweat, red eyes, and dissing a probation officer don't make it likely that a guy is hiding drugs.

The motion's judge thought differently: "There's a standing order in D.C.," he said, "that probationers automatically agree to being searched at any time. This condition of probation waives their Fourth Amendment rights. So law-enforcement officers don't need legal cause to search."

With that rationale the jurist banged his hammer and denied our motion without hearing any argument or testimony. As we walked together from the courtroom, Jake turned to me. "Why are you so smiley, Mr. Campbell? We lost, didn't we?"

"Yes, but the judge may have made a fatal slip, one that an appellate court might overrule. Let's sit down and talk."

I explained the dubious legality of "automatic" waivers, ones not personally agreed to or announced in court. How can one unknowingly consent? These searches hadn't yet been fully tested in D.C.

I added, "Here's our problem. We can only argue on appeal if you're convicted after trial. But at a trial we can't seriously contest the fact you had that meth tab in your slacks. So using courthouse time to fight a slam-dunk case might irritate the trial judge."

"So what? Don't I have a constitutional right to make the prosecution prove its charge?" His question arrowed through the paper bulls-eye of my freedom-law beliefs but then snapped against a courthouse actuality.

"Jake, what you say is absolutely true in theory. But the Constitution cannot nullify a law of human nature. Although he'll not admit it, a ticked-off judge can hammer you at sentencing. On the record he'll insist you need a lengthy term because refusal to plead guilty shows you aren't remorseful or accepting of your guilt."

"That's bullshit, Campbell, and you know it, man."

I felt sizzles from a fancied neon sign above my head. It flashed "FIFTH STREET LAWYER!"— a court-appointed shyster who talked clients into guilty pleas. My words must have seemed like proof I worked for Jake's detested railroad, chugging one way toward grey-bar hotels.

"Jake, I'm sorry, but it's also a reality. My job's to tell you of the stakes involved." Maycore dropped his focus to his just-buffed shoes. I recalled his temper when we met.

"Listen, Jake, don't read me wrong. I'll be glad to try this case and do the best I can. I'm not afraid of ticking off a judge. I do that every day. In fact I'm eager to appeal your Fourth Amendment rights and make new law for you and scores of other D.C. probationers. But you've got to know the risk involved."

"All right, what do you recommend?"

Freedom lawyer paused: *Ah, the age-old client question! It's the easy pitch Fifth Streeters wait for. They knock this ball into the bleachers with their client's guilty plea, then trot around the bases and collect their court-appointment fee.*

In future trials I'd extend more empathy to clients wrestling with this crucial choice of plea or go to trial. I'd respond to their distress when they searched my face for clues: "Mr. Campbell, what would *you* do in my shoes?"

But today I clung to my old freedom-lawyer protocol: *Just explain the options; never push which one to take.*

"Sorry, Jake, it's not for me to say. Attorney ethics leave three choices only the *accused* can make: Whether to plead guilty, ask for judge or jury, and to testify. With that in mind, what do you say?"

"Let's take this bogus beef to trial!" Jake declared. "I'm not riding any railroad to a cell."

"I'm your man," I said con mucho gusto, raised my palm, and smacked my hand with his.

On trial day we were assigned to one of only three freedom judges in Superior Court. Such jurists held constitutional rights above assembly-line efficiency. *All right, warrior whooped, at last a helpful pat from Lady Luck!*

Judge Giles Warfield was a headstrong man I'd stood before as counsel for defense and for the government. Jake and I trudged two flights of gritty granite steps to his court.

Inside I shook hands with prosecutor Lily Sandoff, a former officemate. After Jake was settled at defense's table Lily drew me to one side. "Art, if Mr. Maycore pleads and drops appeal of your motion to suppress, I'll strongly recommend no jail time. We'll continue his probation, same conditions as before."

Although Sandoff didn't tip her strategy, I guessed her office didn't want to risk their automatic Fourth Amendment waivers might get shot down on appeal.

I relayed her offer to my client. At first Jake slumped inside his grey sports coat and slacks, staring at the whorls of oak-grain on our table. Finally he looked up and whispered, "Damn it, Campbell! You just told me of our luck in getting Warfield. Now you're wanting me to plead?"

Freedom lawyer muttered sub-silentio, Maycore, you're getting on my nerves, still questioning my motives, doubting my integrity. You're letting your idealism blind you to the merits of this deal. Yipes— your stance is just like mine was back in student lawyer days!

"Jake, I'm not recommending anything. It's my duty to convey her offer. But you should re-weigh all I said in light of her suggested sentence, one that keeps your status-quo. It's still your call to make."

"And I still want to try this rotten rap," Maycore said with unexpected certainty.

Once my client opted for a trial, warrior didn't shy from urging how to win. "OK, Jake, let's get a jury. No way we can blow away the prosecutor's facts. Our best shot is kindling jurors' indignation when they hear the government addicted you to methadone, handed you a pill, then nailed you for the drug."

"Wait a minute," Maycore said and shook his head. "I'm not so sure of that. You said judge or jury was a choice for me to make. I'm sorry, Mr. Campbell, I don't see this case your way. When do D.C. jurors ever sympathize with addicts? Let Judge Warfield try the case and I'll testify in my defense."

Warrior felt a back-hand slap. "Jake, you might know the mindset of a jury of your peers, but I know this judge. Not even Warfield can ignore the fact you had that pill. Best let me urge twelve folks to let the spirit of the law overrule its letter in this case. But it's your choice. I'll try it either way."

"All rise!" intoned the clerk as Warfield breezed into the court with swirling sable robes. He deposited his lanky six-feet-one into a chair behind the bench and stared in silence at the prosecutor.

Warrior warned, *Watch out! His body language could be either a directive to begin our trial or a dare to mention something he can argue with. Lily and I know firsthand what tiny provocations trigger tantrums from this judge.*

I felt confident Warfield would make Lily prove each drug-possession element and wouldn't punish Maycore for demanding trial for a hopeless case. What I could not foresee was how Blindfold Belle and Lady Luck would join hands to terminate this case.

Lily called her four expected witnesses: Jake's probation officer, both arresting narcs, and the nurse who'd given Jake his morning's methadone.

I cross-examined them with two objectives: First, to show each witness had experience with addicts and could agree with me that methadone was an addictive drug.

Secondly, to tweak the judge's curiosity about why my client hadn't swallowed down his tablet when dispensed. So I asked the nurse and Jake's probation officer, "Wasn't it a fact some methadone-providing clinics closed for the three-day holiday?"

When each answered yes, I asked, "And in your experience wouldn't that create a natural concern among those hooked on methadone that they might not get their needed dose for those three days?" Again they both concurred and I sat down.

Lily rose behind the prosecutor's desk. "Your honor, in the interests of justice the United States will dismiss this charge."

Warrior gasped in disbelief: *Did I just see a prosecutor exercising freedom law?! That's rare as finding ripe road apples underneath a rocking horse!*

"Good use of prosecutorial discretion," Warfield quipped. "I was wondering how I could legitimately find defendant wasn't in possession of that tablet— despite how unfair this prosecution seemed. You've spared this court the problem of how to reach a just result upon hard facts."

Maycore struggled to his feet. "Your honor, am I free to go?" he asked in seeming disbelief.

"You are," Warfield said, then added with a wink, "Next time swallow down that methadone."

Jake turned to me and beamed. "See, Mr. Campbell, I was right to try this case before a judge. But, regardless, thanks for all your help."

By the time I'd shoveled papers in my briefcase's joyful jaws, I figured what had likely run through Lily's mind. It was her last cross-training day, trying crimes in court. Tomorrow she'd return to her old paper-pushing job in Civil Rights.

So Lily didn't have to earn the reputation of a kick-ass prosecutor; she could drop the charge in spite of looking soft on crime. This outcome also meshed with her career to foster people's liberties.

Moreover, Lily satisfied what I surmised were marching orders from her boss: "Whatever you decide to do, don't let that waiver issue reach appeal. We might lose it there."

It was win-win all around: For Lily and her office, for my client, and the District of Columbia— the latter spared the costs of an appeal plus supporting one more boarder in its jail.

As I headed my Camaro home that afternoon, my thoughts dredged up an image that would pull together all this case's quirks. At half-a-dozen places Jake had drawn a different tarot card from Lady Luck.

First he drew a re-addiction ghost, then a freaked-out figure staring at the three-day holiday. This was followed by an unexpected specter in the form of his probation officer.

Next from the deck he pulled a lawyer not afraid to take a hopeless case to trial— and then a freedom judge. But in his final draw Luck turned up a prosecutor whose own stars aligned so she would drop the charge.

Turning off the parkway, I thought of the tagline Jake could scratch beneath our Lady with the Sword: "Governments should not lock up a man for carrying a pill they handed him."

HAD AIN'T NUTHIN'

His poverty, not his will, consented to incur the danger.
— Judge Hawkins, Queen's Bench 1988

The title of this trial is a quote from Rufus Pearl. Years before I was appointed to his case, he'd been a witness for my favorite client, Thomas L. "Cut" Cummings. Moments before Cut's hearing, Rufus and I walked down the courtroom hall. I pointed to a ruby ring on his right hand.

"Oh, this? It's all that's left of my career. Years ago I was a big-band singer. Gigs along the East Coast, snappy clothes, gorgeous women, wads of cash. But I couldn't stay away from alcohol. Now look at me, almost a derelict, barely getting by."

The portly forty-two-year-old in Goodwill clothes stared a moment at the wall, then with a face long as a bus-ride home said, "Let me tell you, what I've learned from all of this: Had... ain't... nuthin'." It struck me as a Zen-like summary of life.

Months later Pearl was accused of robbery and used his one phone call to contact me. Since he was indigent, I secured a court appointment to his case.

Finding him in courthouse lockup, I reached through bars plaqued by years of unscoured paint. Rufus shook my hand. With a smile framed in shame, he muttered, "Now you see what alcohol can do. I wouldn't wish this on a rabid possum."

"I can't see *this* at all," said I, holding up his charging sheet in disbelief. "You're accused of robbery— that kind of thing's not Rufus Pearl. I haven't checked the details but it seems the victim was an elder lady. What the hell went down?"

"I don't know much myself. Last thing I remember it was night and I was sitting on some stairs that led to an

abandoned basement flat. I'd downed a quart of
Thunderbird, the only stuff I could afford."

Rufus cast a forlorn glance behind me as if wishing for
some exit from himself: "Next thing I know it's early
morning and police are putting me in cuffs. I'm lying in a
pile of broken glass inside the showcase of a store on 13th
street. Police said I'd been sleeping with a purse clutched
in my hand. They said I'd grabbed it from some lady on
her way to church."

"Are you sure you can't remember more?

"Honest, Mr. Campbell. That often happens when I drink
too much. I black out then pass out after doing things I
can't recall. I've been busted for shoplifting and other petty
stuff— nothing serious or violent. But how could jurors or
a judge relate to that?"

Unhappily for us, the police account reflected Rufus' words.
The only bright spot was no mention that the victim had
been struck or threatened. She'd only heard footsteps
behind her, then a stranger whisked the handbag off
her arm.

Although this snatching was non-violent it still constituted
robbery, using force to steal property. More bad news: Our
victim's age was sixty-five; judge and jury sympathy would
clearly flow her way.

Next day my investigator rapped on the victim's door.
Maude Crumbaster opened it a crack. As soon as he
identified himself, the lady waved her arms and shouted,
"Get off my porch! You represent that bum that mugged
me. God will punish him and I won't talk to you."

As often happens in the aftermath of crime, victims think
Dame Justice lifts her sword to fight for just one side—
theirs, of course— the side already fortified with cops and
prosecutors. This belief obscures their sight so they can't
see the Lady's blindfold or her double scales.

My investigator brought Crumbaster's words to me. Freedom lawyer felt an itching in his teeth: *How can I fulfill my duty to present a "vigorous defense" in this red-handed case? Silk and scarlet cover harlots but how can I expect a break from jurors when the victim was a senior citizen toddling to church?*

I found my answer tucked inside the trial lawyer's cliché book: "When facts stand against you, pound the law." Technically the law of robbery required more than taking property by force; the taking must result from a *specific intent to steal.*

The police report said Rufus grabbed Crumbaster's purse and instantly fell backwards, losing consciousness. His mind had flown so high in skies of Thunderbird, it couldn't keep him on his feet; perhaps it also lost its tether to intent.

Placing this into a legal frame, Pearl's actions called for an "intoxication defense." Arguably that night his wits became so scattered, they could not align behind the single aim to steal.

The trial took a single day. Before our judge came into court, I shook hands with the prosecutor, Stanley Clithering. "Stanley, we won't fight the fact that Mr. Pearl took the victim's purse. We'll even stipulate that he used 'force' to 'take' and 'carry away' the 'property' of 'another'."

Clithering stepped back as if he needed smelling salts. "I'm not kidding, Stan. I'll state this to the judge and you can tell the jury in your opening if you wish."

"What's left for a trial?" he asked. "I'll try to think of something," I replied.

I saw a woman's eyes discharging daggers at me from the front row of the gallery; their owner matched our victim's profile. Blending tactics with compassion, I suggested, "Stan, why don't you return the contents of her purse to Ms. Crumbaster?" Stanley called the lady forward, let her have the items back.

I waived opening statement. Our defense would surface on the words of Stanley's witnesses. But that plan would only work if no one knew which statements I'd be waiting for.

From voir dire to final arguments my strategy was wholly non-combative. When I rose to cross-examine the complainant, I bowed slightly: "Ms. Crumbaster, I know that occasion must have been traumatic. You have my client's and my sympathy for what you went through...."

From the corner of my eye I saw Stanley rising from his chair to sling a protest at my style. I hadn't followed courtroom protocol by only asking questions; I tossed him a nod.

When he eased back in his seat, I switched to proper etiquette: "Ms. Crumbaster, besides being scared and startled, you weren't hurt, were you?"

A. No, sir, but he took my purse. As I said before, it had my wallet with twelve dollars, a letter from my granddaughter, keys to my apartment, a compact, and other personal things.

Q. And except for the purse itself— exhibit A, resting on the table over there— all its contents were returned to you, isn't that correct?

A. Yes, sir, but not until this morning when the prosecutor gave them back.

With authentic pity I brought out how, despite her fright, Rufus never threatened, touched, or said a thing to her.

Q. Now, Ms. Crumbaster, can we be absolutely clear what happened next? As soon as Mr. Pearl grabbed your purse, he staggered back and tumbled through the large glass window of a store?

A. Yes, sir, that's true.

Q. And after Mr. Pearl landed on the floor with all that shattered glass, he lay dead still, didn't he?

A. Yes, sir, but I was scared to step in there and take my purse. I feared he might wake up. That's why I crossed the street, went into a neighbor's house, and phoned for the police.

Q. Ms. Crumbaster, would you estimate how long it took for the police to come?

A. I'd say about ten or twelve minutes.

Q. During that time did you and your neighbor keep an eye on Mr. Pearl from her house across the street?

A. You'd better bet we did.

Q. And you never saw him move from where he fell?

A. No sir, not until police arrived and raised him up.

Q. Thank you for your honesty and patience, Mrs. Crumbaster. I have no further questions for you. Again I apologize for what you endured.

My cross of the arresting officer finished weaving undisputed facts into a basket that would carry our defense. When he'd approached the scene my client "seemed unconscious." Rufus "came to" only after being shaken by the shoulders and slapped hard in the face.

I began our case's formal phase by calling Pearl to the witness chair. Wearing dark wool pants he'd pressed between some books in jail the night before, he tried to walk with dignity across the courtroom floor. After Rufus introduced himself I asked if he would summarize his stage career for members of the jury.

"Objection!" uttered Clithering, marching towards the judge's bench, a signal we should conference there. "Mr.

Campbell's clearly trolling for the jury's sympathy. This man's career is utterly irrelevant to robbery."

"Not at all, your honor," I replied. "Our entire case rests on an intoxication defense. My client's lack of a specific intent to steal is based upon on the fact that he's an alcoholic. Jurors must hear evidence of this to decide if they believe our claim. They need to know how he became that way— how his career as a celebrity led to his alcoholism."

Seeing hesitation in the judge's countenance, I added, "That's why I stipulated every other element of robbery— to save time for your honor and focus on this single vital aspect of our case."

Judge Slapsaddle raised his ballpoint pen, held its tip above his trial ledger, and declared: "Mr. Campbell, I'll allow a *brief* rendition of your client's history of employment as it relates to alcoholism."

So Rufus was permitted to recap nine years of singing with big-bands, of long trips on dilapidated buses, how booze eased his ride and livened up the motel scene. His recollections seemed a cache he'd stored against indifferences of time.

He'd avoided heavy drugs but gradually the alcohol became compulsory. It maintained his highs on stage and cushioned crushing lows between his gigs.

"Eventually I took a drink as soon as I woke up. I'd go through a fifth of gin or vodka before noon. After singing with the orchestra at night, I'd drink til I passed out. Half a dozen bands gave me second chances to clean up my act. But I couldn't beat the devil in that bottle. So I climbed inside."

Rufus took a breath and slowly let it out. "I haven't held a singing gig for years— nobody will hire me. Yet I can't find the strength to walk away from alcohol."

I moved closer to the jury box. "Now, Mr. Pearl, turning to the afternoon before the incident with Ms. Crumbaster, what had you been doing?"

"I'd been drinking vodka almost that entire day— finishing at least two quarts. That night I spent my final dollars on a bottle of Thunderbird wine. I was sitting in the stairwell of a vacant basement apartment."

Rufus paused, stared out the courtroom window, then his thoughts returned. "I looked back at that stairwell after officers had handcuffed me. It was only twenty feet from the window I fell through. The last thing I remember— before I felt the police slapping me— was finishing the wine and not being able to get up from those freezing stairs."

Stanley's cross-exam of Rufus aimed at proving his last sentence was a lie. He started digging where he thought lay Pearl's softest ground.

Q. Mr. Pearl, when you finished all that alcohol, of course, you wanted more, isn't that right?

A. I don't know for sure. I think my body knew I'd drunk enough. One time I tried to rise up from those chilly concrete stairs but couldn't seem to move.

Q. Come on, Mr. Pearl, isn't it a fact you ran out of booze, needed cash to buy some more, so you attacked a lady with a pocketbook?

"Objection!" I yelled, leaping to my feet. "Ms. Crumbaster never said she was attacked— only that her purse was snagged."

"Overruled," responded Slapsaddle. "Counsel for the government may frame his questions as he likes. It's for the jury to decide exactly what occurred."

Emboldened, Clithering fired questions from all angles— like bees around a honey thief. Quizzing Rufus faster than the word of God, the prosecutor tried to prove defendant grabbed the victim's purse *because* of a specific intent to steal.

Rufus fielded every question thoughtfully, a paradigm of humbleness. Stanley realized his tactics couldn't topple Pearl's sturdy narrative. So his final query sought to strike a stunning blow or spark an overly emotional retort: "Mr. Pearl, isn't it a fact you *knew* you robbed that lady and you're *lying* to us now?"

Far from flashing anger, Rufus grew contrite: "I'm sorry, sir. I can't remember anything about that lady or her purse. I won't deny it happened. And I apologize to her right now. But it was not the real me that took her purse."

"Who *was* it then?" asked Stanley, no doubt thinking he had finally snared defendant in a trap.

Rufus slowly shook his head. "It was the man who'd crawled inside a bottle and completely lost his way."

"No further questions," scoffed the prosecutor, sitting down as if in triumph. But his parting shots, like tired arrows, never reached their mark. Sympathetic juror faces watched my client step down from the witness chair.

Our other witness was a psychiatrist I'd engaged with court-appointed funds. The doctor testified he'd worked for years with alcoholics. He explained how sometimes chronic drinkers in their cups acted like sleep-walkers, managing composite tasks with virtually no consciousness.

He added that these patients often suffered blackouts, blocking memory of their acts. Yes, he had examined Rufus Pearl and listened to his courtroom testimony.

"Based on Mr. Pearl's history and what you heard today in court about his drinking all that alcohol and not recalling what he did, is it your professional opinion that Rufus Pearl is the type of alcoholic who could grab a woman's purse and not know specifically what he was doing?"

"Absolutely, yes," he said.

"Your witness, sir," I said, nodding to the prosecutor.

I expected Stanley's cross-exam to bash our shrink's opinion with the fact he'd not spent many hours with my client. The prosecutor didn't disappoint me there.

He also made our doc concede his views depended on defendant's speaking truthfully to him and inside court today. Then like a bulldog Clithering sprang for our physician's jugular: "Isn't it a fact that your conclusion rests entirely upon Mr. Pearl's self-serving version of the facts?"

"Yes, sir, it does," he said, "but, having worked for years with many alcoholic patients— which include some very clever liars— I believe him totally."

"Your honor, I object!" yelled Clithering. "This man's trying to usurp the jurors' function. Only they can say if they believe defendant's lying."

"Too bad, Mr. Clithering," said the judge. "Your question called for a response." Stanley sat down tight-lipped, shaking his head back and forth.

It was time for our summations to the jury. In rare agreement on one point, both Clithering and I told jurors if they thought Pearl lied to them and the psychiatrist, they should find him guilty.

But Stanley tried to split his stance into another chance to win. He argued, even if our jurors did believe my client's testimony, they needn't buy our expert's theory that Pearl snatched the victim's purse without intent to steal.

It took less than sixty minutes for the jury to return to court from their deliberation room. "Not guilty!" the forewoman beamed. Beneath her blindfold, Lady Justice smiled.

I framed "Had Ain't Nuthin'" and hung it on my office wall.

SAWED-OFF SHOTGUN TRIATHLON

I: SUPPRESSION HEARING

A student asked, "If God is good, why does the world contain evil?" Ramakrishna replied, "To thicken the plot."
— Unknown source

A freezing D.C. autumn thawed to warmth for patrons entering Jet's Liquor Store on 15th Street. Some stood near the heater of this mom-and-pop establishment.

In clumps of two and three they chatted, nodded, shifted weight from one foot to the other, postponing their return to icy breaths and stinging cheeks.

Suddenly the front door on its coiled-wire spring swung open, slamming hard against the wall. Inside stepped a tall man in his twenties and a shorter, stouter man who clutched a paper-handled shopping bag. The tall man reached inside his Navy surplus peacoat and withdrew a sawed-off, double-barreled shotgun.

"Hold it!" yelled the gunman, leveling his barrels so they swept a waist-high arc before the wordless crowd. Patrons turned to statues, mouths agape, gazes fixed upon two hollow eyes of death.

"Give my friend the money from your register!" barked the shotgun wielder. His cracking voice might be aggression, doubt, or fear— but Jet's owner didn't pause to find out which.

A veteran of robberies in this rough part of D.C., the vendor raised his right hand while his left index finger sought the no-sale button on his register. After poking its release, he inched one shoe beneath the counter where it toed a mute alarm.

The drawer ka-chinged against the owner's aproned paunch. He scooped bills from their tiny coffins, hoping

44

he'd not have to lift the drawer and rouse two sleeping hundred-dollars bills.

Still holding high his right, the owner stretched his left hand crammed with cash towards the second man. The bagman grabbed the bills and dropped them in his sack.

"Now lady," said the gunman to an elder customer, "give me that money in your hand— I saw you tried to hide it." She held out her shaky palm and watched him seize a wadded five.

"Nobody moves for fifteen minutes!" the gun-holder yelled. "We'll be waiting just outside." The robbers shuffled backward toward the door. The gunman tipped his weapon up, then tucked it in his coat; both men strolled outside with emphatic nonchalance. The entire episode took less than sixty seconds.

Five minutes later Stanley Spardor and Cullen Graften lounged in the backseat of a taxicab, paused behind a traffic light three blocks from Jet's. Abruptly six policemen, pointing their revolvers, swarmed the cab.

A sergeant at the driver's door yelled. "Everyone, hold both hands in front of you where we can see them. Now... very slowly... exit from this vehicle."

Imagine the reactions: cabbie's, cops' and taxi fares' when a peacoat was discovered covering a sawed-off shotgun on the floor beside a shopping bag of dollar bills.

* * * * *

Spardor was indicted on two counts of armed robbery, two for ordinary robbery (in case a jury disbelieved the gun was real), five counts of assault (scaring) with a deadly weapon, and a final count of possessing a prohibited weapon (shotgun with sawed-off barrels). Graften was indicted as an aider-and-abettor to all of the above.

Superior Court appointed me to Spardor's case. I walked down the courthouse stairs to lockup where I called my client's name. A handsome, lanky, twenty-four-year-old broke from a group of prisoners and abruptly held my gaze with his aggressive stare.

I stuck my right hand through the bars. "Stanley Spardor, I'm Art Campbell, your assigned attorney."

"Skip the Stanley, call me Shaft," he said and crunched my hand. "I know this all looks pretty bad," he added, twitchy as a tickled trout, "but you'll still defend me, right— not bargain me into a prison cell?"

"Sure, that's my job. That's what I do."

"You've got to help me beat this bogus beef. All I did was get into a taxicab and found a gun and bag of money there. Cops said there'd been a robbery. They took me and Graften to a liquor store in cuffs and gathered people all around, folks complaining they'd been robbed."

Shaft looked quickly to one side and added, "One cop held up the coat, the gun, and paper bag with cash. Of course, those dumb-ass people fingered us. They had no one else to choose!"

I stared at Spardor, trying to size him up. Did he think his new attorney— only five years older than himself— would buy this tale as compelling proof of innocence? Was Shaft stupid as a sack of rocks or did he hail from Vergil's clan, "drinking deeply from the vapid cup of hope?"

Shaft had pitched what D.C. lawyers called the "Tyrone defense." Translation: "Some guy called Tyrone must have done the crime." (Californians labeled this the "Soddi defense"— "Some other dude did it.")

"Let me check things out," I said. Seizing something positive from Shaft's rendition of the facts, I added, "If cops planted the idea in those peoples' minds that you and Graften pulled the heist, there's no way your trial can be fair. I might bring a motion to exclude I.Ds of you. If they're knocked out, the only evidence could be fingerprints upon the gun."

"Hell, I know they'll find my fingerprints! I grabbed the shotgun when I found it in the car." This explanation leapt out quick as a cricket— as if crouched and waiting for the chance.

I asked one of my investigators to interview all witnesses who would speak to her. She knew the valediction cops and prosecutors give "their" witnesses: "We're not saying to *avoid* all people representing the defendant. We're just reminding you about your *right* not to speak to anyone who's not from the government."

With that reminder most eye-witnesses balked at talking to a person from defense. Or else they wouldn't sign or scratch initials under any captured words that tumbled from their lips. (By contrast, lawyers in a civil case could subpoena witnesses to their private offices, transcribing reams of answers given under oath.)

Next day my investigator returned. "Sorry, Art. As soon as I told folks who sent me, not a single one would talk. All I got was the police report."

That account declared "there was a show-up I.D. of defendants in the store." But since it didn't mention how it was conducted, I went with the picture Shaft had sketched: All victims had been gathered round my client and his friend, collectively agreeing that the men in cuffs had been the perps.

I plunged into research on unlawfully suggestive I.Ds. My motion to suppress centered on a case that listed ten verboten tactics of police, first among them showing suspects to eye-witnesses assembled in a group. I appended current scientific tests revealing weaknesses and blunders of eye-witness testimony.

As trial lawyers know, people pointing fingers in a courtroom don't identify a person from their crime-scene memories. Instead their minds match faces later seen in show-ups, line-ups, or a photograph-I.D. What's more, in trials they invariably point to anyone who's sitting in defendant's chair.

If cops had staged a biased show-up at Jet's Liquor Store, they'd cause an unfair trial. Because of that, courts set the weight on prosecutors' shoulders to prove I.Ds at crime scenes had *not* been unduly suggestive.

On the day of the suppression hearing Spardor and Graften were bused from jail to court. Attorney Giles Bristlecone had been assigned to Graften's case. Pushing forty, Giles always wore an eerie grin, like a kid who still had all his M&Ms after eating all of yours.

Giles worked on Fifth Street, whose attorneys usually told defendants trials were hopeless and would only get them harsher sentences. They'd assert their client's best chance lay in pleading guilty to some lesser charge— after which, of course, the lawyer could collect his fee from court.

I later learned these types were specialized in California: "Dump-truck lawyers" gathered clients in a group and dropped them onto guilty-pleading dockets of the court. "Escort lawyers" personally led each client to a plea-accepting judge.

As we waited for the motions judge, my client overheard co-counsel recommend a plea to Graften. Shaft turned on both of them and growled, "We're not pleading guilty— no how and no way!" Graften dipped his chin and shrugged. "You heard the man," he muttered to his lawyer.

I exclaimed, "Hold on, guys— don't jump the gun! Let's see which way this hearing goes, what we can learn, what's left of prosecution evidence." Giles, replied *sotto voce*, "Right, Art— it's fun defending clients that have no defense."

Despite the man's sardonic swipe, I knew where Bristlecone was coming from. The man's ambition hacked a clever path through court-appointed clients. Although he pled his

daily dozen into jail, he didn't shirk a trial that might hone
his skills or bring his reputation some acclaim. He used the
poor in hopes that he could sell his talents to the rich.

"All rise," announced the bailiff as Judge Harvey Stormhold
stepped from the doorway of his chamber. A large man
with a booming voice, he enjoyed his reputation as a judge
who put the prosecution to its proof; he was a freedom
judge.

Last time I'd appeared before him I was prosecuting. I'd
won my case but only after crossing every "t." This time,
even with a hopeless case, I believed we'd get a thorough
hearing on our motion, followed by an honest trial.

Our learned opposition was Leon Clapsaddle: early thirties,
ample talent tucked inside a leggy six-foot frame. I'd faced
him once before— in Cut Cummings' final case— which I'd
won by proving his police detective lied in court. Leon still
afforded me respect but I knew his warrior would be
looking for a chance to knock me down.

Clapsaddle herded six eyewitnesses to court. Each took the
oath in turn, described what had happened at Jet's Liquor,
and his or her I.D. of both men cops had brought into the
store.

My cross-examination snagged admissions of how petrified
they'd been; how they'd mainly focused on the shotgun's
barrels or the gunman's trigger finger; how the episode
had lasted less than 50 seconds in a cloud of super-charged
adrenalin.

I covered all this territory without using cards or notes,
changing aim each time an answer edged towards a point
my motion to suppress had listed for the court.

Warrior turned a secret somersault: *What a rush to cross
free-hand!* Freedom lawyer flashbacked to days he thought
he'd never keep his wits intact unless he'd scripted
questions on a yellow pad or notecards: *Art, me lad,*

you've come a long way since you first brushed back
a courtroom bar.

Nonetheless I couldn't get a single witness to admit that
cops had showed defendants to the patrons *en masse* after
brandishing the seized peacoat and gun. Indeed four
witnesses swore police first placed them in the store's back
room, then brought each out alone to see if anyone could
recognize their handcuffed suspects.

Of course this view contrasted sharply with the scene Shaft
had described, the one on which I'd built our motion's
strategy.

Warrior clenched his jaw in irritation: *Did Shaft think I
wouldn't fight if he'd admitted what occurred at the I.D.?
Au contraire, if he'd told me the truth I could have focused
my research and arguments on the real show-up scene.
Not only have we lost that chance but it's ripped our
credibility to assert a flawed rendition of the facts.*

I got two victims to concede their fellow customers *might*
have stood beside them when they'd fingered the accused.
Warrior mutely cheered: *At last, a pinch of credence for
peer-pressure studies in my memo!*

Clapsaddle's final witness was the veteran detective who'd
conducted all I.Ds. The man was certain neither he nor any
cop had trooped through Jet's with gun and coat held high,
implying "Hey, we've got the guys!"

Moreover, he maintained he'd *not* displayed his suspects
within presence of the other witnesses. That would
contradict his training and six years of expertise in
gathering solid evidence for trials.

At hearing's end Judge Stormhold ruled each witness had
performed a valid, isolated I.D. at the liquor store. He
chalked up contra testimony to confusion due to stress.

Bottom line? All six witnesses could testify at trial of their
I.D.s at the store. They could also play the phony ritual

aimed to rouse twelve jurors and the press: pointing out
defendants as they sat beside their counsel in the court.

Stormhold called a thirty-minute recess "before we start
the trial in this case." Two strapping U.S. marshals walked
defendants back to lockup in the basement. Clapsaddle,
looking proud as if he'd wiped out polio, gathered
prosecution witnesses round his desk.

I approached Judge Stormhold's bench, waving off our
court reporter; her record needn't capture my remarks.
"Your honor, can you tell me how I could have brought my
motion more effectively?"

"Well, of course, it always helps to have a firm grasp on the
facts," he grinned, recognizing Shaft had tooled me there.
"But you also sounded too text-bookish. I was put-off
when you tallied ten points of suggestibility like a checklist
for the court. In the future just say how you want me to
assess the facts at hand."

Freedom lawyer thanked him for his feedback and advice.
Walking back to counsel's desk, warrior shook his head:
*But those ten points formed the perfect architecture for
our case.... Oops, I forgot— our job is convincing others,
not ourselves!*

Half an hour gave me time to contemplate the regiment of
evidence arrayed against us. *Holy Santa Anna,* warrior
thought, *Shaft and I are standing on the ramparts of the
Alamo!*

II: KITCHEN-SINK DEFENSE

I think you work a little harder when you're scared.
— Rocky Balboa

Six victims of armed robbery or assault were poised to
point out Spardor as the sawed-off shotgun brandisher.
The weapon, paper bag, the money, and a peacoat that

the gunman wore had been found five minutes later with my client in a cab.

Shaft's would-be defense was that he'd been strolling down the street when the robbery occurred. But the only man who could support this alibi had been found with Shaft inside the taxi and now sat next to him as co-defendant.

So Shaft was staring at ten felonies. Even after rules of double-jeopardy peeled away the overlap, he could languish half a century as a Big House resident.

I groaned when Shaft relayed to me his co-defendant's version of events: Yes, Graften had been present at the robbery but was forced to help the gunman bag the cash. Then by sheer coincidence Graften saw his neighbor Spardor climb inside the taxi when the real robber fled the cab.

Good god, that tale's big enough to swamp a lifeboat! I hope he doesn't drop it on us during trial. But regardless, how can we survive the prosecutor's perfect storm of evidence?

* * * * *

Let me place our pending trial in a different frame. I'd reached the point where people often say, "Art, give up— your guy clearly did it. How can you defend a guilty man?" Cocktail parties were designed to let folks hurl that question at defense attorneys.

After fielding this pitch a hundred times I no longer flinch at the grenade it's meant to be. Instead I grab another chance to share my passion about freedom law. Subject to the patience of my listeners and my level of blood-alcohol, here's what I try to get across:

"I don't act from some perverted love of crime or evil people. I don't defend my clients' *acts* but their *rights* as Americans. I serve the Blindfold Lady and the court for which she stands. Our country doesn't *yet* make people disappear because police or politicians want them gone.

52

Courts don't *yet* brand citizens as criminals because the media persuades us they are bad.

"In America the government must still support its charges publicly with constitutional evidence. If a defendant really did the crime, then it should be provable. To ensure the game's not rigged, the adversary system makes it like a tug of war. Prosecutors yank on one end of the rope while independent lawyers tug the other way."

At this point I check how many of my audience are glassy eyed. If there's still an active listener, I step back on my soapbox:

"But if the defense doesn't pull with vigor on its end of rope, how can our adversary system work? If defense attorneys let the rope fall slack because they think their client did the crime, they'd replace our legal system with their own subjective judgment. They'd become both judge and jury."

I like to finish facing the initial questioner: "You say I'm defending so-and-so, but I'm really standing up for *you*, for *anyone* not yet accused of crime. What I'm defending is our *system*— to make sure *everyone* stays free."

I've spent years fine-tuning this harangue, but it seldom satisfies my listeners. Lay people— even civil-practice lawyers, die-hard D.As, law-and-order judges— rattle ice-cubes in their drinks, nod, and edge away. They prefer to cling to cartoon versions of our courtrooms hung in five-cent frames.

* * * * *

With my client in the cross-hairs of his Gatling gun, Clapsaddle formed his troop of witnesses in one corner of the court. Grinning like a wicked prince, he ambled toward my desk: "Art, I think it's time we talk."

"Sure, Leon. Want to toss an offer on the table?"

"I know you'll stretch out trial for a day or two in your search for specks of doubt to throw in jurors' eyes. I respect your skill and preparation ever since you cleaned my clock in Cummings' case. So, to save the court and government the costs of trial, I'll give you more than usual— surely more than the accused deserves. If Spardor pleads to one count of armed robbery, I'll drop all nine other counts."

Disguising my surprise at this nearly free-pass from the Alamo, I said, "That sounds fair to me. I'll go down to lockup and convey your offer to my client. Tell you his response in fifteen minutes."

"What, you won't *sell* it to him?" cried Clapsaddle.

"Sorry, Leon, I'm not prosecuting anymore and I don't practice Fifth Street law. I won't *sell* a guilty plea— I'll just convey it to my client."

As I've previously confessed, I always felt a painful twinge when plea-pondering clients stared at me with utter faith and asked, "What would *you* do?" My routine response was, "Only you can do the time— so only you can draw the line."

Freedom lawyer felt his duty as an advocate was defending clients, not arranging their surrender. *Moreover,* warrior added, *two years down the road I don't want to see a client's writ of habeas assert: "My lawyer talked me into it!"*

But Shaft's case changed my view. Today the prosecutor's offer towered far above all likely outcomes of a trial. I finally recognized that, after I had earned my client's trust, the most helpful service I could give was genuine advice of when to plea.

Call it "advocate's compassion" unless that gores your oxymoron. Yet, my amended attitude jibed with coaching from my favorite client, Cut Cummings. Although now dead, Cut's baritone still echoed in my mind like actor Morgan Freeman's: "Mr. Campbell, what you need to work on is your empathy: thinking more like other folks."

So today with fresh determination I marched downstairs to lockup. Marshals brought my client to an eight-by-ten-foot conference room with custard-colored tiles, steel table, and two straight-back chairs.

"Shaft, I gave our suppression hearing my best shot. But no appellate court will reverse Judge Stormhold's ruling based on the facts he found— that you were shown to people individually, not all at once. And you know I'll take this case to trial— I told you, that's my job." Shaft eyed me suspiciously.

I continued, "But I can't see a verdict come your way when six eyewitnesses, peacoat, gun, and loot are thrown at us. And you with no defense except the alibi that you'd been strolling one block from the robbery scene."

Shaft raised his chin and squinted cross the cigarette-stained table: "Okay, Campbell, what's the D.A. offering? What's in play?"

"He said he'd drop all charges if you'll plea to one count of armed robbery. Instead of facing fifty years, the max would be fifteen which could mean parole in five."

Shaft slammed his fist onto the table three inches from my arm. "Hell no, I'm not pleading nothing! Let them *prove* me guilty. That's my right. And I demand a jury trial. Are you with me on this, Campbell?"

"You know I am, Spardor. But this time I'm saying you should take the deal."

Warrior rolled his eyes: *We're trapped in no-man's land with overwhelming foes in front of us. Suddenly through all the fire and smoke an exit from the combat zone appears and Shaft won't budge! If he thinks all this is just a game, he'd better check the score.*

Last weekend I'd been reading Carlos Castaneda; now two points leapt to mind. "Shaft, this is your cubic inch of chance. Grab it now or you'll regret it all your life.

Someday you'll die with the totality of who you are. Why not seize some time to *live* with it?"

Shaft stared at me blankly. "Stuff that bullshit, Campbell, whatever it's supposed to mean. You told me once a trial is the client's choice to make. That's what I'm choosing now."

It was folly to imagine Shaft and I had bonded as apprentice-shaman. Even framed as man-to-man, I hadn't earned this level of his trust. Whatever was his strategy for life, it hid inside a box marked DO NOT OPEN NOW.

"OK, Shaft, I'm ready for our jury trial," I said, rising from my chair. I left him with a firm handshake and smile of assurance that I didn't feel.

* * * * *

It was time to rummage through my meager arsenal. To start, I'd try a tactic I'd been saving for a judge with tolerance to entertain a novel argument.

Seeing Leon's empty desk when I returned to court, I set my briefcase there and spread out my materials. It was the table closest to the jury box. Warrior thought, *I always sat here when I represented Uncle Sam. It sent a silent message to members of the jury: Hey, you guys are on my side!*

Clapsaddle sauntered in and looked at me in mild surprise: "Hey, Art, forgotten you're no longer playing on the good guys' team?"

"Leon, you've got the football and the evidence. So I should get to choose my side. Let's see if Stormhold backs me up. Regardless of which way he rules, the other one can raise it on appeal. It's time we get this favored-table issue settled by the law instead of by default."

"Okay, go for it. You've got nothing else."

Both defendants and attorney Bristlecone arrived. When Stormhold entered court he smiled at our switched positions. I stated all my reasons, so we'd have a record for appeal.

"I agree it's time we get some law around this issue, Mr. Campbell— so I order you to change your seat back to the desk that's farthest from the jury. Furthermore, I'll take judicial notice that throughout Superior Court the prosecution almost always gets the desk next to the jury box, even when defense requests to sit there."

Okay, freedom lawyer muttered with relief, *that's one issue for appeal.* But warrior added, *Now we're back to having space between us and our jurors— too bad it won't mute the proof they'll hear.*

Stormhold, Clapsaddle, Bristlecone, and I consumed the afternoon voir diring jury candidates. We questioned over one-hundred applicants— more than normal for a robbery trial— to weed out everyone with prejudice from sawed-off shotguns, threats of violence, or media accounts of robberies.

Five times Leon called a conference at the bench; five times he sang the same refrain: "With all due respect, your honor's being far too deferential to defense's doubts about impartiality of these jurors."

Each grievance edged the judge's temper closer to its boiling point. "Objection noted and overruled for the umpteenth time," Stormhold said while staring out the window at a scrawny maple tree.

Minutes later Leon criticized the judge again. Twenty-three surviving juror candidates dropped their jaws as Stormhold pushed back in his swivel chair and roared: "Mr. Prosecutor, this court has lost its patience at your persistent niggling and insinuation I'm not being fair! I hereby dismiss the entire panel. We'll start over in three days. This court stands adjourned."

Leon's face was livid but he wisely vised his mouth, staying rooted to the floor until the judge had disappeared behind his chamber door.

Spardor called me over to his chair behind our desk. "Right on, Campbell now you've got him on the run!"

* * * * *

On day three we rose again while Stormhold took his throne. Instead of letting counsel for defense and prosecution voir dire new potential jurors— only fifty had been sent this time— Stormhold did the questioning himself.

Hoping not to tweak his wrath, I objected "only for the record" that defense could not participate. "Noted, Mr. Campbell," said the judge. "Now you have another issue for appeal." In one hour Stormhold chose twelve jurors plus two alternates, sworn "to well and truly try this case."

As expected, Leon rallied his parade of soldiers, split them into squads of I.D. witnesses and cops, the latter armed with sawed-off shotgun, peacoat, paper bag, and cash.

Cross-examining the victims, I swung the same axe that had scored some glancing blows at our hearing to suppress. It chipped some flakes of doubt from contradictions about where the various participants had stood inside the store.

I chopped a few more slivers from the dimness of the lighting and under-sixty-seconds observation time. And, of course, I hacked away at victim-fear, getting every eyewitness to admit that fright could cloud her view and memory of that life-threatening episode. I let all these fragments pile up beside the witness chair.

I kicked myself for making one mistake— until I righted it next day. Clapsaddle planned to call the co-defendant's ex-girlfriend; she hadn't testified before. But the able prosecutor had to seek a conference at the bench because he couldn't recollect her name.

I chimed, "It's in my notes at counsel table. I'll get it for the court." I stepped away and dug it out— completely missing Leon's proffer what she'd say. Next day, to my dismay, I learned.

The witness— big-boned, twenty, perfect teeth— informed the jury, "Cullen Graften bragged to me last month that he and Shaft had robbed Jet's Liquor Store."

"Objection!" I yelled, jumping as if epée'd by a cattle prod. I quick-stepped to the judge's bench; Bristlecone and Leon joined me there.

"Your honor, they're a dozen cases that condemn the prosecution's implicating one defendant with confessions from another."

"Those only outlaw statements by *police*," said Leon, "not layperson witnesses."

"But it has the same colossal prejudice on jurors," I replied.

Stormhold shook his head and said, "Mr. Campbell, we held a conference yesterday to clarify this matter. You made no objection whatsoever at that time."

"That's because I never heard what she would say! If you recall, I'd stepped to my desk to help this court locate the woman's name. Now that she has blurted out her prejudicial statement, at least the court should let me call the co-defendant to the witness chair. That way I can confront my client's accuser, the one who placed him at the scene."

"Mr. Bristlecone," said the judge, "does the co-defendant wish to waive his Fifth Amendment right and take the witness chair?"

"Yes, he'll waive his right, your honor," said Bristlecone, nearly silent up til now, "but only for the purpose of refuting this alleged 'confession'."

But warrior was still spinning in an eddy flanked by Scylla and Charybdis: *If I don't call Graften, I'll miss my chance to jimmy up his girlfriend's nail in Spardor's coffin. But if he takes the witness chair and tells his cockamamie tale about being forced to help the real robber, he'll seal that coffin with a giant screw!*

Three lawyers moved back to their oaken desks. I peered at the wood-grain whorls, searching for an answer to my tactical dilemma. Happily for me, Judge Stormhold called a halt: "Ladies and gentlemen of the jury, court's adjourned until tomorrow morning, ten o'clock."

I raised my chin and brows to the approaching marshals as I pointed to my client's chest, then mine. They granted my implied request to talk with Shaft before they packed him on their steel-shuttered bus to jail.

Shaft and I agreed he shouldn't testify. Jurors knew he'd been arrested three blocks from the robbery scene. But except for Grafton— and his far-fetched account— Shaft had no witness to support his bony alibi that he'd been merely walking down the street when Jet's robbery occurred.

By next morning I'd decided Graften's explanation for the words to his ex-girlfriend would help more than hurt our nearly hopeless case. But worries of what else he'd say led me to forget to call him to the witness chair.

That blunder struck me when I said, "Defense for Mr. Spardor rests... oh, except for one more point. Your honor, may I reopen briefly?" Stormhold sprinkled mercy from his gavel, let me summon Graften to the witness chair.

As feared, the co-defendant's price to help my client was his chance to sell the jury his own unlikely tale. "I was *at* Jet's store when it got robbed but I'd been taken *hostage* by the gunman just before. No, it wasn't Mr. Spardor. The *real* robber jumped out of our cab when Mr. Spardor got inside."

The hostage yarn was welcomed as a wuffle from a wounded water buffalo. I scanned two rows of jurors; each face was clamped behind a stolid neutral mask.

Graften tried to clarify the so-called "confession" to his ex. "That woman got my words messed up. All I said was me and Spardor had been *charged* with robbing Jet's Liquor Store."

Sound convincing? warrior asked. *Not to me,* said freedom lawyer, wishing he were somewhere else.

Time for final arguments. Leon started first, stalking back and forth before the jury box. "How could there be a stronger case against two men than what you've seen the last two days?"

He went on: "Six victims stared right at the gunman and his cohort, then from the witness chair each one identified these co-defendants. Police told you both men were arrested within five minutes of the hold-up, three blocks from the liquor store. And with what? The peacoat, sawed-off shotgun, and the cash they stole!"

As Leon piled on each crushing fact, I stared at the grimy courtroom window. At first I tried self-hypnosis: *Hey, just wait until I tell the jury all about our winning case!*

When that failed I recalled my private ethics trinity: I owed duties to my client, to our adversary system, and to freedom law: *Regardless of the odds, you must present a "vigorous defense." Okay, time to launch the kitchen sink.*

When prosecuting months ago, I'd tried a case of deadly battery, using just two victims' oral testimony. In defense's final argument, my opponent asked the jury why I hadn't brought some scientific evidence to court. My counter— "Did I need to wheel in the kitchen sink?"— provoked the jury's answer: "Yes!"

In private papers I had called this argument the "kitchen-sink defense" and noted its potential clout. Now as a last resort it seemed handy as a hidden pocket. The night before, I'd rehearsed it with my fiercest critic, Dru.

Today when Leon finished and sat down, I rose and boldly strode to a spot before the middle of the jury box. My eyes made seriatim contact with each juror's gaze. Then warrior, feeling like a gladiator left with only one small dagger, raised his weapon in a pose of desperate self-assurance.

"Ladies and gentlemen, if the government's so sure that Mr. Spardor is the man who robbed Jet's Liquor Store, why haven't they shown you the kitchen sink?"

I paused to let the jury's puzzlement roost upon that phrase. "My learned friend has thrown a lot of things at you, everything *except* the kitchen sink. So where's the *rest* of his potential proof?

"Where are *fingerprints* to link my client to that gun? Doesn't their omission make you wonder, give you doubt backed by a reason? As Judge Stormhold will instruct you, 'doubt backed by a reason' is what the law calls reasonable doubt."

I continued jabbing at Clapsaddle's unpresented evidence. "If the government's so sure that's a *real* shotgun, capable of shooting real shells, why have you not seen ballistics evidence? Indeed, why has the government failed to show you any *scientific* proof my client is the guilty man?"

Walking to the far end of the jury box, I pivoted. "And while we're listing missing dishes from the kitchen sink, why has the government not produced the taxi driver in this case? Don't you want to hear from him if Mr. Spardor had been *wearing* the peacoat and *carrying* the gun and loot when he got in the cab? Maybe those things had been dumped inside the cab by someone else. How *did* those things get in the mystery taxicab?"

Warrior started feeling confident, finding new momentum from hearing his own words; indeed he talked for twenty minutes without notes. He yoked the absence of potential evidence to slight differences between six witnesses' descriptions of the hold-up. He ended by connecting all his kitchen-sink of doubt to studies of inherent weaknesses of eye-witness testimony.

To my surprise the jury huddled for six hours, then returned complaining it was deadlocked with no unanimity in sight. *Alright,* warrior whooped, *we'll count this as a victory!*

Judge Stormhold summoned all three counsel to his bench. "Mr. Campbell, do you wish me to declare a mistrial or exhort our jurors to deliberate some more?"

Freedom lawyer strategized: *Somehow a maverick must have slipped inside the jury box, a holdout who refused to bellow "guilty" with the herd. I don't want that juror to get worn down by more deliberation until he turns his vote against my client.*

I asked co-counsel Bristlecone if he agreed that we should seize the mistrial opportunity. "Yes!" he answered instantly. Then Leon surprised us: "The government joins in the motion for a mistrial."

Warrior felt this like an uppercut: *What does Leon know? Why would he fear more deliberation by our jury?*

Before I figured out a motive for the prosecutor's odd endorsement, Stormhold cleared his throat and said, "The court declares a mistrial in this case. Thank you, ladies and gentlemen, for your attention during trial and your attempts to reach a verdict you could all agree upon."

Then the judge leaned forward and dropped his voice. "By the way, I'm sure counsel for both sides would like to know how many jurors favored a guilty verdict. Does your foreperson care to share that information, now that trial's over?"

A forty-something man with coat and tie rose from the front seat of the jury box. He emitted a long-suffering sigh: "Nine of us felt both defendants were not guilty."

Shock rocketed around my head and plunked squarely on my face. Shaft tugged my jacket sleeve. Looking happy as a pool of dolphins, he said, "See, I told you not to take the deal!"

Later, when post-morteming this bizarre result with Bristlecone, we agreed the kitchen-sink defense— dropped on Leon far too late to call a plumber— must have poked some doubts in what had seemed his solid case.

Why did Leon also want a mistrial? Once more Bristlecone and I concurred: The prosecutor didn't want to risk a verdict for defense when he possessed the kitchen sink to throw at us next time.

III: SCUMMIEST LAWYER IN D.C.

Law is what we live with.
Justice is sometimes harder to achieve.
— Arthur Conan Doyle

On retrial Leon trundled in his kitchen sink, crammed with all the items he had previously left out. Besides cops and six eye-witnesses, our second jury pondered fingerprints, ballistics, glossy pictures of Jet's Liquor Store, and aerial photos of the six-block scene.

Clapsaddle also called the cabbie to the witness chair. The man swore co-defendant Graften had first hailed him, then a moment later Spardor climbed inside. The driver listed every street he drove his fares along until his taxi was surrounded by gun-pointing officers. With a map at counsel table, I ran my finger down each street he named.

Two defensive tidbits hid inside the cabman's testimony. I hurled two grenades to blow them out. Each was risky but this was crunch time; maybe one would blast some doubt into Clapsaddle's case.

Q. Sir, you *didn't* testify that you saw Mr. Grafton or my client with a shotgun or a paper bag— is that correct?

A. Yes, that's correct.

Q. To be absolutely truthful, that's because you didn't *see* either man get in your taxi carrying a gun or bag— isn't that also true?

A. Yes, sir, that's true.

Warrior furtively let out his breath: *Whew, no blowback from that one! Those questions might have jogged his memory, let him toss another frying pan into the sink!*

My next grenade just blew some puzzlement into the prosecutor's case. On direct exam the cabman had apparently confused the sequence of the roads he'd traveled with his fares.

On cross I asked him "as a licensed expert of our city's streets" to repeat the order of those roads. When he complied, I asked, "Are you absolutely sure that was the route you took?"

"Yes, sir," he answered with a scowl of in-your-face.

I invited him to step down from the witness chair. Would he use my felt-tip pen and trace this route upon Clapsaddle's aerial photograph?

As I repeated each street in the order he had named, jurors watched him sketch his progress with a wobbly line. His route crossed itself three times— his curlicues a tangle of perplexity.

Later in the trial I stood to chuck a third grenade of doubt, this time against one robbery victim's prior words. But as I drew back my arm, the bomblet blew up in my face. Let me sketch some background, showing how its pin fell out by accident.

Judge Stormhold had docketed our second trial to start the day before Thanksgiving. Clapsaddle, Bristlecone, and I jointly importuned him to postpone the opening until Monday following the holiday. All three of us were scheduled for reunions with our families out of town.

Half-masting bushy brows, the jurist said: "Counselors, you may have Thanksgiving Day. The courthouse will be closed. But on the day before and after, you belong to me."

All three lawyers were upset— and didn't hide our sour faces— but what else could we do?

Enter last grenade. When Clapsaddle finished questioning a victim of the robbery, I wanted to exploit the person's former contradiction about where he'd said both robbers stood. Maybe I could detonate a crack in Leon's sink.

Hurriedly I leafed through four transcripts spread across my desk, trying to locate the inconsistent statement this man made. I wasn't sure if it occurred at the preliminary hearing, before grand jurors, during the suppression hearing, or at our prior trial.

Stormhold cleared his throat. "Your witness, Mr. Campbell. Are you ready to proceed?"

"Just another moment, if it please the court. I need to find a document." Finally I unearthed his statement from our previous trial. But the transcript's cover lacked a date to show exactly when his statement had occurred. Protocol demanded I identify the time and place at which a witness made a prior declaration, so the person could recall if it was made.

To avoid more loss of time, I decided I would satisfy the protocol without mentioning the date.

I stood up with the transcript in my hand. "Mr. Blankenship, did you not testify in this case's prior trial that the gunman was...

"Mr. Campbell!" boomed Judge Stormhold, "get up here right now!" All three lawyers scurried to the bench. The jurist was as livid as a shaken can of bees, but he kept his voice low so the jury couldn't hear his words.

"Mr. Campbell, you're the scummiest, most unprincipled, unethical lawyer it's been my misfortune to see practice in the District of Columbia! You've told the jury of a former trial in this case, knowing how extremely prejudicial it would be. You did it deliberately, to provoke a mistrial. That way you could leave for a Thanksgiving vacation which this court has ruled you may not have!"

My warrior was engulfed in smash-mouth fury: *Judge, you've got a vicious case of gavel-mind— outrageously judgmental— banging out your blame on the assumption other people are as devious as you!*

Knowing my career was gone if I let warrior free, I torqued his arm to elevate my shield. I'd need protection on the record if Stormhold tried to hold me in contempt of court.

"With all due respect, your honor, that's preposterous. As you can see," I said, handing him my sheath of papers, "there's no date on this trial transcript. I was merely orienting the witness to his prior statement, as I must, before I used it to impeach him. Besides, where's the prejudice?"

"No you don't, counselor!" Stormhold angered on, barely holding down his decibels. Despite my doubt the jury could make out his words, it was clear the judge's wrath was aimed at me.

"Now that jurors know your client's had a prior trial, they'll surmise he wasn't guilty. That's what you telegraphed and that's exactly why you told them. You knew they'd get so prejudiced against the government, I'd have to call a mistrial."

My pulse shot even higher. How could Stormhold— who'd known me for years— so misjudge my motives or morality?

Freedom lawyer tugged my sleeve: *Maybe he forgot to take his medicine today. He's known for these explosions on the bench. "Off his meds" is what folks usually say about his unexpected flare-ups.*

But Stormhold's vicious epithets had struck home— more so from the fact he was a freedom-judge. When he brushed aside my honest explanation, I could scarcely hold my rage.

Feeling my throat filling up with feathers of adrenalin, I inhaled deeply and replied, "Your honor, I believe we'd better take a brief recess, so both court and counsel can calm down."

"Denied, Mr. Campbell! Now let's all get back to work."

Stormhold turned to the jury box and in a grim tone warned twelve very curious watchers "not to draw conclusions from the mention of a prior trial in this case or speculate on what has just transpired at the bench."

Then, in systematic refutation of his rant about my sewing prejudice, he lectured them about "the myriad events that could have caused a second trial, the one you're sitting on today."

He concluded, "Now this court's adjourned until 9:30 Friday. Have a nice Thanksgiving Day."

* * * * *

It was tough to celebrate Thanksgiving with Stormhold's accusations gnawing in my gut. Plus I had to think of what to say next day for Spardor's final argument.

I rehearsed again with Dru, once a public-speaking champion in the state of California. She advised I start by thanking jurors for their patience and attention throughout trial.

She warned me not to point to any tiny spoons of doubt
rusting at the bottom of the prosecution's overflowing sink.
"Indeed," she cautioned, "this time don't say 'kitchen sink'
at all."

After two belabored practice hours, Dru tried to lighten
up my mood. "Remember, Art, the rodeo ain't over til
bullriders ride." But her image roused a different thought.
I said, "Tomorrow, looks like bull is all I've got."

In court on Friday, I tried looking nonchalant as Leon
catalogued his mass of facts for members of the jury. He'd
filled his kitchen sink with every type of evidence known
to the forensic world.

Once more I stared at the courtroom's mucky window.
Sunlight, trying to break through, made each pane a film of
tired shellac. When my turn came to argue, I tried shaking
off the gloom and clambered to my feet.

"Ladies and gentlemen, there are many stains of reasonable
doubt upon the surface of this case. I'll not take your time
by listing every one because I'm sure you will remember
them yourselves. I'll just mention two."

Placing the aerial photograph on an easel before them, I
pointed to the spider-web of contradictions shining from
criss-crosses of the cabbie's felt-tip marker. I also asked the
jury to recall what I'd pried loose from one victim's
contradicting others about where the "real culprits" stood
inside Jet's Liquor Store.

In all I gave it my best shot, melding Dru's advice with
classic arguments for raising doubt. But when I resumed
my seat I knew I hadn't fired any potent shots— while
Leon's mass of nails, nuts, and bolts were blasted from a
giant blunderbuss.

No one was surprised one hour later to see jurors troop
back into court. "We find both defendants guilty on all

counts." Themis, blindfold justice goddess, finally got to rest her weary arm.

After our last juror straggled out and bailiffs took away defendants, I approached the bench. Stormhold's prior censure still stuck to my ego like a piece of gutter gum. "Your honor, yesterday after you berated me in court I went home and talked about it with my wife."

I turned and gestured to Drusilla, who was sitting in the gallery's front row. She'd come to take the measure of a judge who'd dare attack her man. But when Stormhold gave a cordial nod her way, she flashed her million-dollar smile. Instantly the jurist's face converted to a boyish grin.

I continued, "Judge, my wife can pull deep-rooted weeds out of my mind, but she barely talked me out of handing you my lawyer's card today. That's how upset I was that you would think I'd stoop to what you said I'd done. You made me want to quit the law."

Stormhold shrugged his shoulders as he answered in a jovial tone. "Oh, Art, forget about that 'scummy lawyer' thing." He curled his index fingers round the phrase, as if to soften it with quotes. "I spoke in the heat of the moment— just lost my cool. You've seen it happen other times in court. Don't take it personally."

As the jurist blithely thrust my torment to back-burners of his brain, warrior reeled: *Whaaaat?! How many lawyers get called scummiest in town— on the record, by a judge— and simply shrug it off? Who* <u>*can't*</u> *take that personally?*

Since I'd first appeared before a justice of the peace in law-school days, I knew litigation called for egos harnessed inside battle-toughened hides. As lawyer for defense and prosecution, I'd endured my share of tirades from the bench. But being branded "scummy" and "unethical" had pushed warrior to his tipping point.

In pre-law days my fighter would respond to words like that with fisticuffs. Could I now restrain his pent-up rage?

70

Then I felt Cut Cummings' ghost beside me. It placed his large palm on my arm: *Pick your battles, Art. Can't you see this one is done?*

I stepped back and drew a breath. Freedom lawyer swiftly leapt between my warrior and his wrath: *Stormhold can't admit it on the record but yesterday he must have missed his meds. Remember, just before his outburst, he was sweating like a glass of ice-tea in the sun? Now he's trying to bridge the rift. Take his offer, let this go, chill your burning spurs.*

* * * * *

Next month Stormhold laid a lengthy prison term on Spardor and his co-defendant. So closed a twice-tried case that could have ended with an advantageous plea.

What did I take away from all of this? To view the world with more intensity through other peoples' eyes: those of clients, co-defendants, jurors, and a judge. To push for guilty pleas when they're appropriate. To use the kitchen-sink defense where timely— knowing what can happen if that sink gets filled. And to grow a thicker skin.

MURDER IN THE FIRST DEGREE

Murder is nothing more than common assault
with unfortunate consequences.
— John Mortimer

Most people suffer without the catharsis of meaning.
— Jane Hirshfield

It was nearly freezing in D.C. when Wick and Crandon
Thatcher ushered Wanda Hazlitt into Ramsey's Bar and
Ribhouse on Sixth Avenue.

Wick was twenty; his cherubic smile beamed from a sturdy
frame of six-foot-two. Crandon, handsome, twenty-one,
walked beside his brother. Wanda glided like a fashion
model, stride for stride behind the two.

"Hey, boys, where're you going with that tasty fox?" yelled
someone at the bar. Fury shooting from his eyes, Crandon
wheeled to find the voice. The speaker, male, fat, and
middle-aged looked like a brick with hair.

Wick's face also flushed with anger but he grabbed his
brother's arm. The two walked slowly to a corner table
and sat down. Wanda, acting as if nothing happened, took
a chair between her two escorts.

The bar-stool patron yanked a wad of bills from his shirt
pocket, waved it in the air, and looked toward Wick and
Crandon: "What, you think you got the stuff to treat her
right? Tell that walking rainbow she should leave her baby
boys and sit here with a *man.*"

Wanda vainly reached for Crandon's arm as he pushed
back his chair and started towards the guy, Wick right
behind. A burly bouncer intervened before the brothers
reached the bar. "Take it easy, guys. Let me handle this. It's
over for that jerk."

Crandon shoved his shirt-sleeves up, shot a slit-eyed glower at the shouter, and resumed his seat. Wick mutely mouthed "Mutha-fucka" at the heckler and sat down.

The bouncer made true on his word. With a forearm come-along he escorted Loudmouth to the back door of the premises and shoved the man outside. "Saddle up your horse before you start a rumble here," the doorman said. The fellow answered with a racial epithet.

Wick and Crandon stared into their plastic-coated menus but they couldn't scrape those taunting echoes from their minds. Wanda tried to calm them down: "Forget it, guys. That drunk was crazy as a roadside crow."

The brothers glanced at one another; Crandon then asked Wanda to excuse them for a men's room call.

The restroom's opaque window— half-way open— peered into a lightless alley leading past the bar's back door. Standing just outside, the ex-patron spotted Wick. "Hey, boy, what's the matter? Did I scare the crap out of you?"

Crandon didn't say a word, just exited the restroom, turned right, then slammed through the bar's rear door. Wick followed on his heels.

What happened next was never made precisely clear. A police report claimed this version came from Wick: "The guy came at us, so we had to knock him down. When he tried getting up, perhaps I left my sneaker on his neck too long."

The bouncer only tacked a coda on that scene: Fat man on his back unconscious amidst scattered twenty-dollar bills, Wick and Crandon standing over him. Paramedics came but couldn't get the fallen man to breathe. Rushed to the nearest clinic, he was D.O.A.

Neither Wick nor Crandon tried to flee. When police appeared they tallied up one fallen patron, empty wallet, and the littered cash. Slapping handcuffs on the Thatchers, cops booked each for strong-arm robbery. When police found out the victim died, they added felony-murder, i.e., murder in the first degree.

Since neither brother could afford a lawyer, D.C. court appointed counsel for both men. A Fifth Streeter was assigned to Crandon. Lloyd Kadish, my fellow graduate student at Georgetown Law, was assigned to Wick.

"Hey, Art, why don't we co-counsel this? Our first homicide, I know— we'll have to work our tails off. But think how much we'll learn."

I thought of nothing else all day. By the time I coaxed my battered old Camaro through traffic to our cottage in Virginia's countryside, I'd sorted through the issues— pro and con— to spread before my household guide.

• Con: Was it ethical for two under-thirty lawyers who'd never tried a murder charge to undertake this case? Could smarts and super-diligence make up for lack of murder-trial expertise?

• Pro: Don't all homicide attorneys try their virgin case? Despite its scary sound, a murder trial uses the same skills that Lloyd and I have been honing since we clambered up a law school's stairs. We can always get advice from veterans, even call one in if something plunges us below our depth.

Dru robustly cross-examined me on all these points. "Looks like the pro's win out," she said.

Warrior wondered, *Does my wife know how easily she reads inside my mind? Each evening I walk through the kitchen door, she spots some secret worry stranded on stalagmites in my brain. Someday maybe I'll learn how to read inside hers too.*

The clinching point for Dru and me? Although Wick Thatcher stared at life-incarceration, at that time his charges didn't lug the penalty of death. Our client would not die if Lloyd or I screwed up.

The court appointed me co-counsel to Wick's case. Walking back from court, Lloyd said casually as if Thatcher had been charged with petty theft, "Let's get Wick out of jail. Isn't he an indigent confined because he can't afford to post ten grand? Doesn't our Constitution say every person has a right to bail?"

"Absolutely," I replied, "and if cats were clouds the sky would mew." I flash-backed to my student-lawyer days when I'd struggled pitching Lloyd's same argument in a state supreme court.

Then warrior pierced my hesitation with a lawyer's maxim: *Art, remember law in court is what is boldly said and plausibly maintained.*

So I changed my attitude. "Okay, Lloyd, let's go for it. Won't be easy bailing out a murder-one defendant on his promise to return. It would be a first in Washington, D.C."

Our investigator scoured the Ribhouse scene, securing witness statements from bystanders, cops, and medical recruits. Meanwhile Lloyd and I researched the law, compiled facts about Wick's life, and drafted bail arguments.

We began with an attack upon the trial court's decree that set bail at $10,000. That approach would free a man with dough but kept Wick Thatcher caged. After ascertaining he was indigent, the court deprived him of two fundamental privileges: every person's right to bail and a poor man's right to equal justice under law.

We appended documents to show our client satisfied each statutory element for bail "on defendant's own recognizance."

First, the accused was born in Washington, D.C. and had lived his whole life there. Without a husband's help, his mother raised him and two siblings. Wick had garnered decent high-school grades and had no criminal arrests.

Next, defendant's fellow worshipers at church and his neighbors called him "gentle and peace-loving." His boss at the Holiday Inn signed a statement touting Wick's reliability. Finally, a respected bail organization gave its written promise to assume third-party custody if a court freed him from jail.

After filing our motion, we scheduled oral argument before Judge Arnold Tyrespiek; he was the jurist who'd set our client's bail.

The judge was a careful courthouse navigator, pulling on his oar so he'd create the least amount of waves. He also had a law-and-order tilt; his robe was frayed from leaning toward the prosecution's side.

At the hearing Tyrespiek exclaimed, "What, let loose a man accused of murder?! Let's see the prosecutor's file." He thrust out his open hand.

Ramsey Crackfield, Assistant U.S. Attorney, looked surprised but rallied with these words: "Your honor, we'd be glad to let the court review our work product *in camera,* but it should not be part of the public record or made accessible to the defense." He closed his file's inch-thick wings, balancing its cardboard spine inside his palm.

Freedom lawyer mused: *Another tag-team, judge and prosecutor, wrapped inside a God complex. It's blinded them to what they've just injected in this case: a new constitutional issue. Lloyd looked at me and raised his brows; I raised my chin to semaphore him back.*

"Judge," said Lloyd with evident concern, "if you're going to base your ruling even partially on what's inside the government's file, due process mandates counsel for defense should see it too. How else can we refute the prosecutor's stack of unsupported and self-serving facts?"

Crackfield, unaware he'd whacked a hornets' nest, blandly argued on: "Your honor, the defense should *never* be allowed to paw through prosecution's file. It contains our strategies, confidential leads, legal theories, and potential arguments. Under the *Jencks* case, defendants only get the statement of a *witness* from our file— and only after that one *testifies* at *trial*."

"Counsel," chimed in Tyrespiek as if calming squabbling kids, "I only want to glance a moment at the file— right now, at the bench. I must assess the danger of releasing Mr. Thatcher."

"Same objection," stated Lloyd, glancing at the court reporter to make sure her fingers pressed the silent keys that snagged these statements for appeal.

Noiselessly my warrior scoffed: *Tyrespiek, can't you find a rationale inside your mind? Why pull something from the prosecutor's bag of prejudice? You're so wishy-washy, if you stopped outside a storefront window, your reflection would walk off with someone else.*

Crackfield handed off his folder to the bailiff. The slow-moving man, khaki uniform merging with his leathered skin, hefted it atop the judge's bench.

His honor opened up the file, lifting papers pinned by poke-and-bend-back clips so he could scan the pages underneath. It took two minutes to complete his peer and ponder task. Then he loosed his legendary will of mercury.

"Defendant's motion is denied for the same reasons bail was set initially."

Tyrespiek was referring to the boilerplate D.C. judges typically invoked when asked to grant non-money bail. This legal-speak asserted: (1) the charge itself reflects defendant's unreliability; and (2) the past has shown non-money bonds are insufficient guarantees.

Lloyd and I marched to our office where we thrashed out how to pitch our points to the appeals court. The fact that Tyrespiek relied on secret evidence now let us highlight all our arguments with due-process paint. We hoped this glow behind Dame Justice would attract appellate scrutiny.

Since bail appeals didn't merit oral argument, we had to wait and see what judgment would descend from legal skies. Nobody held his breath. Seldom did the D.C. Court of Appeals rule in favor of a citizen charged with blue-collar crime.

Next week the appellate holding caught us by surprise. It reversed Judge Tyrespiek, directing him to make a choice: Reconsider non-cash bond or make available "a complete statement of the nature and circumstances of the arrest."

A concurring opinion decried Tyrespiek's "mechanical repetition" of reasons for denying bail, noting "other cases have revealed this rote."

The concurring jurist also took to task the trial judge's use of evidence not shown to the defense: "Fundamental constitutional rights cannot be subject to such dilution."

Indeed, the concurrence stretched beyond six-hundred words, spelling out exactly how our client's bail *should* be set. It reminded Tyrespiek that under D.C. law "no financial condition may be imposed to ensure the safety of any other person or the community."

Its conclusion dropped a heavy hint: "On remand, I would hope that further consideration will be given to the question of non-financial conditions of release."

Tyrespiek didn't need another moving finger on the wall; one concurrence was his trial court command. Next day he released our client on his promise to return.

For a moment Lloyd and I enjoyed the status of celebrities among the defense bar: "What, two post-graduate students

freed a murder-one defendant on his own recognizance!?"
We'd made new law in Washington, D.C.

Freedom lawyer whooped and dialed dinner reservations; it
was time to celebrate. But our triumph was short-lived. In
fact our victory set the stage for tragedy that would
transform our client's life.

Wick dutifully complied with all conditions of his bail:
Worked his job five days a week, slept at home, and
checked in daily with the bail agency.

Meanwhile Lloyd and I prepared for trial. We filed motions
to suppress our client's statements to police, for advanced
discovery of prosecution evidence and witnesses, and for
funds to hire a shrink to study Wick.

The last request arose from clues we'd spotted after
peppering Wick's prior schools and hospitals with
subpoenas duces tecums. (Rough translation: "Under threat
of punishment, you must produce designated documents.")

We suspected Wick might suffer from "organic brain
damage," a now-outdated term for mental functioning
impaired by trauma or disease. We needed confirmation
for potential use at trial.

Lloyd and I were buoyed by another fact: the Thatchers
were the only living witnesses to what happened at the
fatal alley scene. That would leave the prosecutor with a
circumstantial case. To jurors we could liken Crackfield to
a spider knitting wind— attempting to create connecting
strands from his imagination.

But as trial day approached, Wick met his tragic
rendezvous with fate. Perhaps he bought a bogus bit of
street law: "Hey, you're facing life in prison— they can't give
you more than that. Early birds may get the worm but it's
the second mouse that gets the cheese. So why not break
the law again? As far as sentencing's concerned, your
second crime would be for free."

While out on bail Wick got busted for another robbery.
The victim wasn't injured, nor was any weapon used. But a
second robbery charge was serious— and this time backed
by non-defendant witnesses.

With one stroke Wick had blown his personal recognizance
and demolished his defense. No longer could we ask a jury
of his peers to see him as a peaceful or brain-damaged kid,
forced one fraught night to act in self-defense.

Of course we asked Wick why he got entangled in another
crime, but he only bowed his head. Mute as a mummy, he
looked like a kid who longed to shed his last two months
like hazy wisps of binding cloth.

Above our client's silence thundered Lenin's truth: "Certain
facts are unavoidable." No lawyer in the land could make
Wick's second robbery disappear.

Lloyd and I hashed over options to combine both charges
into one negotiated plea. After lining up strategical
alternatives, we strode to Ramsey Crackfield's office.

The prosecutor smirked as we walked in the door: "Well,
well, what goes round *does* come round," he said. After
small talk over sips of brackish coffee, we explored
potential pleas.

Eventually the three of us agreed— subject to Wick's
consent— that Crackfield would dismiss the second
robbery accusation if our client pled to murder-one.
Far from a freebie felony, the latter charge cost Wick
his chance to fight the first.

Our only hang-up was the sentence both sides would
propose. Warrior whispered in my ear, *Life's uncertain; ride
your best horse first.* So I proposed the Youth Corrections
Act. Wick should be imprisoned in a rehabilitation
program that would free him when his age reached
twenty-one.

Crackfield shook off my suggestion like a wet retriever: "Art, you must be joking. That amounts to only one year for a murder!"

"Look, Ramsey," Lloyd stepped in. "We've known you since we were assistant U.S. attorneys. You always were a kick-ass guy but not a knee-jerk one. Let us do more digging into Thatcher's background and come back to you. Give us a chance to prove that justice in this case— for our client and the District of Columbia— lies in a Youth Act sentence."

"Dig away," Crackfield answered with a backhand wave, "but don't cling to any hope I'll change my mind. Whatever facts you find will only slap some icing on a cupcake made of dung."

Lloyd and I drove to jail that afternoon. Two guards patted down our clothes and tilled their fingers through the papers in each briefcase. They led us to a conference room, a ten-by-ten-foot lair tinted beige and sealed by a flaking steel door. Inside sat a wooden table and four metal chairs.

Two other guards brought Wick inside, removed his hand-and-ankle cuffs, then left the three of us alone. We went over all our trial options, then explained Crackfield's offer. Wick readily agreed to the negotiated deal.

In two weeks he'd plea to murder-one and Crackfield would dismiss the second robbery charge. The judge would sentence him one month from then. Meanwhile his attorneys would switch from trial preparation to a full-court press to win a Youth Corrections Act conclusion to his case.

Lloyd and I began an urban archeological expedition. With Wick's sister as our guide, we unearthed more school records, job reports, and letters from Wick's relatives. We scoured everything for proof about our client's naïve personality. We asked Wick's teachers, priests, employers, neighbors, friends, and family to pen letters we could lay before Crackfield and the judge.

We drew on all the energy we would have used for trial to amass an in-depth documentary of Wick Thatcher's life. Lloyd and I discovered there's no traffic when you go the extra mile.

In most cases a defense attorney's job is making clients come across as real folks, not just headlines linked to crimes. Effective in a trial, the importance of this duty doubles in the realm of sentencing. Lest stereotypes or dogma rush to fill vacuums of facts, those deciding others' fates must know precisely whom they judge.

Lloyd and I composed a mini-PhD on Wick. We showed how his character and case made him a classic fit for Youth Act disposition. We chose words and arguments most likely to persuade our client's judge for sentencing: Creighton Bickelhoney.

This jurist was refreshingly devoid of blatant bias toward the prosecution's side. He also topped my list of intellectuals among judges in D.C. He'd give serious attention to our Memorandum in Aid of Sentencing.

To make sure our facts were accurate before we filed the memo, we sent Wick a draft. Freedom lawyer wondered, *What will he think of our attempt to shrink his life to words inside an inch-thick document? Will he be aware of what his lawyers know too well: These paragraphs could steer his future, where he'll eat and sleep and live for years?*

On our next visit Wick said, "The memorandum's fine. Thanks for all your work." So we filed our memo with the court, dispatched a copy to Crackfield's office, and scheduled an appointment with the prosecutor two days hence.

This time Crackfield met us at his door. "God, I've never seen such work by counsel on a client's sentence— I can't believe you guys once were prosecutors!"

Suspecting this hors d'oeuvre was offered on a sharpened knife, I asked, "Does that mean you'll join our recommendation for a Youth Act sentence?"

"Sorry, no can do. I talked it over with my boss. He said— I quote— 'The U.S. government can't back a one-year sentence for a murderer. The media would beat us like a drum, shower venom on this office, ruin both of our careers'."

Disgustedly I uttered, "Politics trumps justice once again! I've heard all serpents thrive til sundown— did he even deign to *read* our memorandum?"

"No, he only thumbed a couple pages. But I studied every paragraph— impressive, I must say. It just might sway Judge Bickelhoney."

"Well, then," said Lloyd, quick to seize an opening, "Let me ask you this. If you can't endorse the Youth Act, suppose the government takes *no* position on Wick's sentence? You'll not offend your boss, inflame the press, or compromise your morals. Just stand mute— let justice take its course."

Crackfield paused to scan the framed diplomas on his wall. Finally he said, "Well... okay. I'll just state, 'The government prefers to let the court decide'."

All right! signaled my co-counsel's wide-eyed glance at me. I smiled and we crunched Ramsey's hand to seal the deal.

On sentence day Lloyd and I made sure Wick's sister— with other members of his family, friends, and neighborhood— was sitting in the front row of the gallery. Their presence and expressions of concern would telegraph community support.

As the bailiff hailed Bickelhoney's entrance, Wick clambered to his feet and braced his thighs against one wooden edge of the defense's desk. Lloyd and I arranged ourselves on either side of him, trying to impart the strength of steadfast bookends.

The judge's gleaming pate dangled sliver fringes down its sides. He eased his slender frame into a leather swivel chair, his expression drawn more solemn than its usual façade.

"Mr. Thatcher, have you read the lengthy memorandum on sentencing your counsel put together for you?"

Wick cleared his throat and answered nervously, "Yes, your honor."

"Are there any facts or arguments with which you don't agree?"

"No, you honor," Wick replied, shifting from his left foot to his right.

"Do you have any complaint about your counsel or how they've represented you?"

"No, sir. I'm very satisfied with all the work they've done."

"You know they made new D.C. law about bail in a murder case?"

"Yes, sir," our client said, then abruptly looked down at the floor.

"I must confess," said Bickelhoney "at first I was surprised your lawyers dared suggest a Youth Act disposition of your case. That would mean one year's confinement for a very serious crime. Then I read about your background and outpourings of support from your community. It appears some of these people are present in the court today."

Wick turned around and flashed the gallery a sheepish smile.

The judge continued, "I'll also admit there came a point at which I was persuaded the Youth Act would be a proper sentence in your case, even for the crime of murder."

Bickelhoney shook his head. "But what changed my mind was your charge of another robbery. Although the government has officially dismissed that case, I can't be blind to the report about that crime. Naturally your lawyers downplayed its significance. But it was the single fact that tipped my mind away from giving you a Youth Act sentence."

Now it was Lloyd and I who dropped our heads and scrutinized the floor. We knew what had to follow that remark.

The jurist cleared his throat, moved a paper on his bench, and looked at Wick. "Unfortunately, once I've put aside a Youth Act disposition, the mandatory-sentence statute leaves me no discretion. For the crime of felony-murder I must incarcerate you for at least a term that runs from ten to twenty years."

Gasps flew from the gallery. I heard Wick's sister moan, "Oh, my god, please, no…"

Patiently the jurist waited for this tumult to subside. "Mr. Thatcher, do you have anything to say before this court passes sentence?"

Lloyd and I had counseled Wick about this moment. Terrified as most folks are of public speaking, he'd told us there was no way he could make a speech. But we'd convinced him he at least could say two words. Thatcher spoke them now.

"I'm… sorry," Wick declared with genuine emotion, looking Bickelhoney in the eye.

"I'm sorry, too," replied the judge. "Now this court sentences you, Wick Thatcher, to incarceration as per D.C.

statute, chapter 22, section 2401, to a term of no less than ten and no more than twenty years in federal prison."

Wick sagged on his feet; his chin fell on his chest. He bit his lip to hold back tears I saw form in his eyes. Two U.S. marshals in freshly ironed uniforms strode to a spot one arm's length behind the three of us.

"Your best hope," said Bickelhoney with manifest compassion "is to be a model prisoner and earn parole in seven years. This court is now adjourned."

"Good luck, Wick," Lloyd muttered as a marshal dropped his hand on Thatcher's shoulder. The other one snapped steel shackles on his wrists.

Although mentally prepared for this result, I was too emotional to talk. Freedom lawyer reeled at the irony: *Our memo walked Wick to the edge of liberty!*

Warrior tried distracting me with biting wit: *That's very true, my friend— and if wishes were fishes, our nets would be full.*

Marshals led our client out the door. It was the last time I laid eyes on Wick.

Lloyd and I shoved papers in our briefcases, turned, and walked back through the gallery. Half-hearted hugs, back pats, and words "you did your best" were parting shots for members of Wick Thatcher's team who'd planned and worked and hoped for all those weeks.

* * * * *

EPILOGUE: Twenty-one years later I grabbed my jangling San Diego phone. A federal judge's clerk was calling from D.C. He'd received a habeas corpus from Wick Thatcher. Did I remember him?

"Of course," I said. "Why's he still in prison after all these years?"

"Well... er... our problem stems from a filing glitch in D.C. Superior Court. They can't locate records for the disposition of Wick Thatcher's case. Neither can the office of the U.S. Attorney for D.C."

"Incredible!" I said.

"That's why I'm calling, Mr. Campbell. Mr. Thatcher's habeas claims there was a plea agreement in his case and the government reneged. He argues he's now being held against the law."

"What makes more sense to me," I said, "is that he's served the statutory max of twenty years for murder and should be released upon that ground."

The clerk said, "Well, that's something else I'll have to check. But I'm calling you to ask if you have any records of a plea negotiation on behalf of Mr. Thatcher. I just got off the phone with Mr. Kadish in Chicago but he says his records were disposed of years ago."

"So were mine. When I moved from Washington I stored my client files where I'd worked with D.C. Law Students in Court. I left the usual instructions to destroy them after seven years."

"We were afraid of that," the clerk replied. "Can you recall from memory if you reached a deal with the prosecutor?"

"Only that he'd drop a second robbery charge if Mr. Thatcher pled to felony-murder— and that he'd stand mute on sentence disposition. Does that help?"

"Not much, I'm afraid. There are other legal issues that I can't discuss, but they're much tougher when we can't locate a record of exactly what transpired in Superior Court."

"Well, I'll look around and call you if I find or think of something else," I said.

I dug through my old notes, ones recording what I'd learned from all my trials. But I'd kept nothing on Wick's case because it never went to trial. Phoning Lloyd, we reminisced about the case but neither of us jogged the other's memory beyond what's written here.

That leaves questions for the ending of this tale. Why was Wick locked up beyond the max of twenty years? Did this once-peaceful youth somehow botch his chances for parole? Did he get tooled by inmate gangs, become involved in prison crimes that welded more years to his life of latticed steel? Did another prosecutor breach some later deal?

One aspect of Thatcher's case is clear. He joined countless casualties of mandatory-sentencing, a brainless feature of our country's "war on crime." It's based on the blind belief that one size should fit all— despite a world of vastly different individuals.

In Thatcher's case the law hamstrung his judge and paved Wick's way to middle-age behind barbed-wire barricades.

Do we ever know enough about our fellow beings to forecast where they'll be two decades hence? Of course, time is an all-consuming god. But Wick Thatcher's case left traces I can't shake about a man-child I once knew.

FURTHER FREEDOM-LAW ADVENTURES

No man is above the law— and no man below it.
        — Theodore Roosevelt

Years before I earned my law degrees, I dreamt someday I'd be a sole practitioner in San Francisco. My full-color vision involved offices with Berber rugs and walnut walls. While still in the District of Columbia some non-trial clients fueled this fantasy. They're depicted here.

* * * * *

Throughout this trilogy I've mentioned lessons learned from Thomas L. ("Cut") Cummings, my favorite client in book one. The following incident occurred not long before he died.

At home one sizzling summer eve in Virginia's countryside, Dru and I were set to make the 30-minute drive to D.C. and a party with some friends. I snatched our jingling kitchen phone. The deep voice inside was unmistakable: Cut.

"I'm sorry to bother you, Mr. Campbell, but 4th precinct cops just busted me for ADW [assault with a deadly weapon.] Some guy jumped me in an alley, so I opened up a can of whoop-ass and karate-kicked him to the ground. But cops checked my record and decided they would call my shoe a 'deadly weapon.' Can you come down and stand my bail?"

"No problem, Cut. Dru and I will be there in an hour." When we arrived I related my intention to a frazzled duty sergeant. Too busy to attend me, he pointed to a bench along the wall. Dru and I sat down beside a dozen other citizens with Friday-night demands.

Fifteen minutes later an assistant sauntered to our spot. Looking at Dru's au courant snug blouse and leather mini-skirt, he asked, "What happened, baby— someone knock you up?" I looked away and tried to stifle my guffaws. Outraged at the time, Dru now laughingly recounts his jive.

Cut? Of course, we bailed him out. Later I got statements from eye-witnesses; his kick was clearly made in self-defense. I convinced a prosecutor it would "serve the cause of justice" if she dropped the charge. Foreseeing loss at trial, she decided to appease the Blindfold Lady earlier.

"Hot damn!" I roared, phoning this result to Dru. "What a rush to use my skills to help a friend and bring a little freedom law to alleys in D.C. Wouldn't it be neat to do this kind of thing in San Francisco?"

"I'll always back that dream," the former Californian said.

* * * * *

My willingness to try what seemed like hopeless cases sometimes switched the calloused butts of prosecutors into offering abnormal deals.

One day the court assigned me to a man accused of three armed-kidnappings. His indictment sounded like police had nabbed a major public enemy.

In truth my twenty-something client merely made three members of a rival gang climb inside his van and dump their weapons on his floor. He drove them seven blocks, then let them go.

For that vigilante act he faced three terms of life-incarceration, plus twenty-five more years— a bizarre result of mandatory sentencing.

I worked up the case and told the prosecutor I was eager for our trial. Result? He tossed in his hand— promised to dismiss all charges if my client pled to one count of attempted robbery! Since that crime contained a three-year max, my elated client seized the deal.

* * * * *

Not long after, the police accused a feeble-minded man of kidnapping two women in their twenties. His neighbors felt a co-defendant must have duped him into climbing in the kidnap car. They could not believe their gentle law-abiding friend could be a criminal.

Folks in his community rounded up the funds for his defense. They tugged an urban grapevine for a lawyer and my name tumbled down. Their leaders trooped into my office, introduced themselves, and stacked piles of twenty-dollar bills along the front edge of my desk.

I leaned back in my swivel chair and tried to look blasé while they recited what they thought had been the real facts. Moved by their confidence and cash, I'd see what could be done.

After documenting the defendant's low I.Q., I secured signed statements from both victims that he'd merely been a passive rider in the perpetrator's car. Negotiations with a prosecutor, followed by a lengthy sentence memorandum, led to the ensuing scene.

The accused and I were sitting at defendant's desk waiting for the judge. At twenty-six my client had a boyish look in his new slacks and natty brown sports coat. His constant grin suggested furniture was missing from his upper rooms.

His neighbors occupied the courtroom's front-row bench, mute witnesses of support from his community. "All rise!" growled a grizzled bailiff as Judge Giles Warfield entered with a flourish of his robes and assumed the jurist's chair.

I'd worked up a Clarence Darrow speech, hoping it would nudge the judge to clemency. Centering my weight, I opened, "May it please the court…"

Warfield—quick to squelch another's thunder on his stage— grinned and cut me off: "Mr. Campbell, it took me quite a while to absorb all twenty-seven pages of your memo. Is there anything you'd like to add before I place your client on probation?"

Freedom lawyer cheered: *Great Scot, he bought my written arguments before I even brought the heat!* Warrior elbowed me: *Careful, Art, don't blow a winning case with a provoking oral argument.*

My compliant silence spawned a festive anti-climax. Warfield ordered one year of probation for defendant, banged his hammer, and sat back on his throne.

My client's friends rushed forward to embrace him. "Praise the Lord!" one whooped. "Praise Mr. Campbell too," another said. "He got probation for a man accused of kidnapping."

From many points of view this was a humdrum case. Like scores repeated every day throughout a lawyer's world, victory didn't burst from pyrotechnics in the court; it grew from conscientious work behind the scenes.

But for me this minor triumph marked a time to celebrate. I'd labored hard to earn my fee, practiced freedom law, and helped a blameless kid go free. If I could do it in D.C., why not some day in San Francisco?

* * * * *

A stifling sun stretched out one D.C. afternoon. Beyond my air-conditioned office, people slouched along the summer sidewalk as if slogging through high-definition hell.

I'd jackknifed my body in an office chair, reading law books splayed across my desk. Glancing up, I glimpsed two figures staring at me from the threshold of my door.

One was a lady in her forties, less than four-feet tall. Her plump arms gripped the handles of a partner's wheelchair. In it slumped a withered man whose age was tangled in the ravages of gravity and time— my guess ricocheted between forty and sixty years.

Their ragged outfits tagged them both as front-line soldiers in the ranks of city poor. As I stood up, the woman boldly wheeled her vehicle to a spot beside my desk.

In a husky voice she said, "I'm Greta Lee Bentwhistle. This is my companion, Broken Lance. I'm a Little Person— he's a Cherokee. The F.B.I. are shooting us with radio waves, urging us to do some crime, so they can lock us up in separate cells."

Despite the weirdness of this tale, I figured they were harmless clingers to beliefs that lent some meaning to the fears of their chaotic world.

"Ms. Bentwhistle, I think I understand the situation but what do you think *I* can do?"

Until that moment Broken Lance was as inactive as a hibernating bear. But now he raised his head and spoke with rock-hard timbre: "Mr. Campbell, we were told you were a different kind of lawyer. We want you to make them stop." His unwavering gaze confirmed his confidence.

My mind raced to find some link between my own reality and theirs. "Let's see what I can do," I said and reached for my telephone.

Knowing Dru had gone to work, I dialed home and let our phone continue ringing as I spoke: "F.B.I.? This is Art Campbell. Yes, the lawyer. Please connect me to J. Edgar Hoover right away."

I waited seven seconds for my phantom then-director of the F.B.I. "J. Edgar? Art Campbell here. I've got two clients in my office whom you've made the targets of your secret do-a-crime campaign. Only it won't work against them anymore— they're onto you. What?..."

I pressed the receiver hard against my ear as if listening to objections, frowned, and then said, "That won't do, J. Edgar. There's only one way you can stop me from exposing your entire scheme— cease broadcasting messages to Greta Lee Bentwhistle and her friend Broken Lance."

Pausing a few seconds, I concluded with "You will? I have your word? Okay, J. Edgar. Bye for now."

My pro-bono clients were ecstatic. "Thank you, Mr. Campbell! We can finally get some peace." With new vigor Greta wheeled her partner down the hallway, back to life upon the streets.

Oblivious of consequences, I bragged to office staff about my 30-second fix for folks whose plight appeared unsolvable. Too soon I reaped the harvest of my phone call scheme.

For weeks thereafter people straggled, skulked, and sauntered up to our receptionist, some sporting caps of wrinkled foil. "I'm trying to ward off signals beamed by agents of the government. I heard Mr. Campbell has a way to disappear these voices in my head."

For each I reenacted variations of my faux conversation. But, like trying to repeat a miracle, my later F.B.I. calls seldom seemed to have the first one's clout. When I hung up, most clients simply shook my hand and shuffled off in the same haze through which they had appeared.

Perhaps I'd let my own conviction drop a notch, knowing colleagues in adjoining offices had their ears cupped to my wall.

Eight months later Dru and I were car-bound, caught in D.C. traffic, wondering why four lanes of autos next to us had lurched to sudden halts despite green traffic lights.

I let my foot out on the clutch to speed ahead of them— and nearly battered two pedestrians whose heads were bobbing lower than the hoods of cars. It was Greta wheeling Broken Lance. With daredevil grandeur they paraded past five traffic lanes against the light!

When I told Drusilla who they were she rolled her eyes and shook her head. I said, "Hey, they're one reason why your husband went to law school— to wedge a little difference in a world that shuns, enslaves, or slaughters its diversity. Wow— to think our Yellow Bird nearly mowed them down on Thirteenth Street!"

There was more support for hopes someday I'd have a San
Francisco solo practice. One came from an earnest lawyer-
client. I was striding down the hall, enroute to arraignment
court, and felt my arm grasped gently by a short man in a
costly three-piece suit. He looked thirty years of age.

"Mr. Campbell, you don't know me but I've been arrested
for protesting our most recent war. I'm a tax attorney and
heard that you were good in things like this. Can you help
me out?"

"What exactly is the charge?" I asked. "Refusing to leave the
White House Grounds," he said, not hiding the anxiety that
pinched his face and voice.

Through work outside a courtroom's door, I arranged his
plea to the lesser crime of disorderly conduct. This was
coupled to dismissal of the White House charge, plus
advance approval of probation. Finally, when my client's
probation term expired, the government would not— and
did not— fight my motion to expunge all public records
of his crime.

* * * * *

Occasionally I'd visit court to see what I could learn
observing other lawyers. Tongs and hammers often flew
in pretrial motions brought to block illegal evidence. As I
fished for practice tips, sometimes I questioned whether
prosecution warriors— doggedly resisting every move the
defense made— had pondered their strategic costs of
victory.

Years later I saw two seasoned prosecutors in the du jour
"trial of the century." For days on nationwide TV they
fought a pretrial battle for admission of a leather glove.
Refusing to concede its doubtful constitutionality, they
finally won permission to admit the glove in evidence.

But at trial they had to introduce it by a racist cop who
claimed he'd found it at the murder scene. Result? Jurors

stared as a celebrity defendant strained in vain to fit the glove onto his hand.

Later, defense arguments harped upon the bigotry that might have tainted it as well as other prosecution evidence. Jurors, riding waves of reasonable doubt, set O.J. Simpson free.

This verdict set off groans from talk-show hosts and pundit lawyers, shaking fingers at a "monumental miscarriage of justice." But my warrior and my freedom lawyer saw it differently:

Prosecution lawyers simply blew that case. Their blind determination to block every move by the defense got their glove in evidence. But they failed to foresee how it would dominate the larger picture— one hand clapping, as it were. They gave defense the race card that it played to win the game.

* * * * *

Returning readers to D.C., my eagerness to litigate sometimes wore down the judiciary. One day I moved the court to sever a defendant's traffic charge from his accusation of grand larceny.

My client, forty-four-years old, allegedly had boosted goods from an electronics shop. Cops swore they'd only stopped his auto for a "routine traffic stop." When they asked to see his license, what he showed them had expired. Cops later popped his trunk and found it crammed with stolen merchandise.

On its face my motion wasn't strange; courts routinely sever minor charges from more serious ones. But my reason was distinctly unconventional: The U.S. Attorney had failed to present the traffic count to a grand jury.

What sustained this wild claim? The statutory sentence for expired licenses was "no <u>less</u> than six months incarceration." Logically those words permitted life in prison; that would constitute a felony, requiring grand-jury action as a constitutional guarantee.

My motion bristled with a dozen points of law; I risked judicial wrath for litigation overkill. I'd aimed constitutional cannons at the molehill of a traffic charge. But freedom lawyer also honored canons of attorney ethics that required me to "mount a vigorous defense."

Judge Wilfred Bournemouth was assigned to rule upon the motion's merits. A literal paragon of blind justice (his clerks read everything aloud to him), he was known for his keen intellect and wit.

On hearing day I set my briefcase on defense's desk but let my notes doze peacefully inside. Because I'd raised such arcane arguments, my strategy was to seize whatever point had caught Judge Bournemouth's fancy and try to shift it toward my client's goal.

When Bournemouth took the bench he praised the motion's novelty. Warrior noiselessly exhaled: *At least he didn't junk it and berate me for consuming courthouse time*.

For fifteen minutes the jurist sparred robustly with me over law and history of the U.S. Constitution. But when time came to rule, he gave the reins of freedom law a special shake.

Rather than prolong a traffic charge by making it parade before a grand jury— or let me pitch my logic to appellate courts— Bournemouth said, "Counselor, I will not deny or grant your motion. Instead I'll step around it."

He continued, "I judicially construe this traffic statute so that 'less' means 'more.' Hocus-pocus, Mr. Campbell! Have I not just saved your client from potential life incarceration for driving on an expired license?"

What else could I do but join in court-wide laughter?

* * * * *

In those days defense attorneys dreamt they'd someday land a Perry Mason case. That's where counsel proves in court a prosecution witness did the crime. Thanks to Ron

Rogers— a Perry Mason sleuth par excellence— my career came close to netting one of these.

I'd been hired by the mother of two teenage boys accused of snatching jewelry from a senior woman on a nearly empty bus. The victim hadn't seen who'd grabbed her watch and necklace, but another teenage passenger said he'd watched it all go down. He even volunteered the robbers' names.

My slim soft-spoken clients— never been arrested, both with passing high-school grades— were charged with multi-counts of battery, assault, and robbery. As juveniles, they could be confined in kiddy-jail til their age hit twenty-one.

Dimitri Hogworth, nicknamed "Hoggy," was the prosecution's sole eye-witness to the crime. My investigator Ron, a law-student volunteer, was sure he could persuade the victim and her witness to communicate with him. I wanted their signed statements of the incident.

Digging for his quarries in an inner-city neighborhood, Ron struck lawyer's gold. First he discovered Hoggy's girlfriend, Grace, innocently adorned with the purloined necklace. When Ron informed her of the robbery she was naturally upset.

But when Ron added that the loot contained a diamond watch as well, her good-grief switched to fury. "Hoggy gave a diamond wristwatch to Latina yesterday! Of course, she never told me where she got it— she knew I was Hoggy's *real* girl."

Ron secured signed statements from both outraged femme fatales. He assured them that their temporary silence would result in zesty vengeance once his boss (yours truly) unmasked Hogworth in the witness chair.

On trial day Ron drove both ladies to the court; their purses clutched the hot accessories as evidence. I went over their intended testimony and invited both to wait upon an oaken bench outside our courtroom's door. That's where I made my big mistake: They perched there for anyone to see.

Hogworth wandered by, spotted them, and jumped like he'd stepped on a rattlesnake. With an ashen face he quick-stepped to the prosecutor's office and confessed.

Both brothers and their mom were thrilled when the prosecutor dropped all charges. Ironically the WASHINGTON POST stuck this outcome in a back-page paragraph, much smaller than its prior story linking my two clients to the robbery.

All I could do was let my warrior daydream how news media might have trumpeted this Perry Mason case: *If only I'd been sly enough to hide our dynamite til Hoggy sat down in the witness chair!*

* * * * *

Next spring freedom lawyer felt another surge. The American Civil Liberties Union asked if I would represent four women housed in Lorton Prison on the outskirts of D.C. They were charged with seizing one wing of the penal complex, as part of an attempted inmate takeover of the facility.

The U.S. Attorney's office had subpoenaed them to testify about the episode before a grand jury. I learned five other inmates had spearheaded the revolt; they were the bulls-eye on the prosecutor's target. But my clients risked extended prison terms if they refused to talk about the incident.

After checking out the facts and law, I spent half-a-dozen hours parleying with prosecutors. I was able to secure complete immunity for my four clients. In exchange for truthful testimony, they'd be safe from any charges that arose from their part in the mutiny.

This little triumph triggered a surprising second victory. My clients' evidence disclosed what lay beneath the insurrection— many disregarded long-term, inmate grievances. So, despite insistence by the prosecutor, the grand jury wouldn't bring indictments against any prisoner in the protest takeover.

Reflecting on these episodes, I realized my scope of freedom law had grown beyond encounters in a courtroom. I'd learned to penetrate the courthouse smoke and mirrors. Now I could negotiate with folks who jiggered levers of the law inside the wizard's lair.

CROSSROADS

We must be willing to get rid of the life we planned,
so as to have the life that is waiting for us.
— Joseph Campbell

During D.C. years I worked twelve-hour days. Litigation ruled my life like nothing had before. My conscience told me timeouts longer than a weekend were just self-indulgent luxuries compared to what my clients faced.

Even weekends at our cottage in Virginia's countryside saw my concentration leap-frog from the problems of one client to another. *Am I prepared for all appearances in court next week? Should I dig deeper for more facts? What new legal research might I do? Have I filed every useful motion? Have I found the most effective strategy? Is there a novel theory I can wrap around this case?*

Drusilla joked about my "file-folder mind," the way I focused totally on one case, then jumped to another with the same intensity. What we both realized— but couldn't yet discuss— was my inability to walk up to my mental file-cabinet and slam shut all its drawers.

One day I felt doubts about the trial-lawyer life rattling in my consciousness. Fidelity to freedom law had not slackened one iota but my soul began to feel frayed. Had I been whumped by litigation burnout?

This happened long before I'd learned about the subtleties of workaholism. Since I wasn't ready to acknowledge this disease, a short-term tonic would have been a little rest and relaxation. But I brushed aside this simple remedy. Refusing to accept fatigue and stress, I treated them as threats to my self-image and career.

I called a summit with my warrior and freedom lawyer to get their views on my misgivings: Freedom lawyer propped his chin onto his knuckles for a moment and then said: *There must be attorneys who can savor courtroom highs and other victories enough to suffer through the never-*

ending search for facts and law, prepping strategies and arguments, shifting calendars and tactics, dealing with eccentric judges, handling unreliable witnesses and erratic clientele.

Warrior asked, *What happened to the joie de vivre that used to thrust its muzzle out our old Camaro window on the drive to work— like some blissed Dalmatian speeding to a fire?*

Freedom lawyer sighed: *Nostalgia sure ain't what it used to be! But, seriously, you nailed it— somewhere we've all lost our fire-dog enthusiasm. I'm not sure if Art's a real trial lawyer anymore.*

As I look back upon this time, it's clear I'd let my loyalty to freedom law completely justify my workaholic life. Learning how to make things happen in a courthouse made me feel powerful and needed. Moreover these preoccupations served to stiff-arm existential fears and risks of real intimacy— even with my wife.

With the fervor I employed to argue for defendants, I had rationalized my duty-bounded life: *Sorry, can't take time for other things— clients must come first.* Only later would I realize I'd trapped myself inside a toxic paradox: Pursuing freedom for my clients, I had given up my own.

Doubts stepped up their nagging when I quit my post as Special Assistant U.S. Attorney and notched an LL.M from Georgetown law. But I responded like a classic workaholic—let a "geographic" redirect my energies.

Asked if I would take a teaching job at D.C. Law Students in Court, I promptly answered Yes. This was the country's premier legal clinic, sponsored by five law schools in our nation's capital. So my workaholism found a different hideaway inside its host: I wouldn't have to face a virus I refused to recognize.

The change to clinical professor seemed quite natural; I still walked to court. But now I went as backstop for law

102

students whose court-appointed clients had been charged with misdemeanors or served by landlords with eviction notices.

Some defendants' dwellings teemed with rats and roaches under leaky roofs, wrecked doors, and broken plumbing. When our clients dared complain about their squalid premises, slumlords filed suits to kick them out.

I helped students learn to document these facts, draft pleadings, garner witness statements, and prepare for trial. So armed, they learned how to bargain win-win settlements or litigate against unlawful evictions.

The joy of teaching took me by surprise. In return for sharing what I knew about a courthouse and the law, I relished learning what I could about my students' lives and how they viewed the world. I was gratified to find their sense of justice resonated with my views of freedom law.

Students also helped me nurture empathy. Not much older than my scholars in their final law-school year, I remembered all too well my fears of public speaking, blundering in court, or ruining a client's life.

In our office I ran seminars on law and tactics, facilitated client conferences, and counseled pupils one-on-one. In court I made sure no clients suffered from a slip-up by their student lawyers. After court I critiqued pupils' actions, helping them improve their talents and reframe their experiences in the most constructive way.

For two years I enjoyed a sense of in-the-trenches comradeship, the way pursuit of expertise and justice bonded students, staff, and lawyers. As we battled slumlords gouging indigents, my range of freedom law enlarged.

To provide a positive example and improve my skills, I represented sundry clients of my own. Prior pages of this book depicted ones I thought most interesting.

* * * * *

One day the editor of a major law-book publisher flew in
from New York and took me out to lunch. Earl Kellett
asked if I'd expand my Georgetown master's thesis on
probation to a treatise on the law of sentencing.

"We need it to complete our series in the Criminal Law
Library. Your book would sit on lawyers' desks next to
ones by current legends F. Lee Baily and Henry Rothblatt."
I laughed good-naturedly, "Who, me? Apart from lethal
boredom— sifting through ten-thousand court opinions on
what happens *after* people are convicted— where would
I find the time?"

Earl answered like a seasoned advocate. "Art, you seem to
savor teaching clinically. Why don't you land a *normal*
teaching job, not this time-consuming one? You'd love it
and the law-school scene would give you opportunities to
write. You said you haven't had a real rest in years. As a
full time prof, you'd get three months annually. Please, give
some thought to this idea."

Drusilla and I spent hours mulling over all the pros and
cons of Earl's offer. By this time Dru had earned a masters
in communication from American University. She loved her
job as host, producer, and on-air personality for D.C.'s
affiliate of National Public Radio.

But from childhood Dru had itched to be a novelist. And I
still fantasized a solo San Francisco practice. Perhaps Earl's
plan would bring us closer to our dreams.

Freedom lawyer gave the thumbs-up sign: *You'll get a total
break from litigation's sturm-und-drang and give your
irritating doubts a chance to sample some alternatives.*

Warrior likewise pitched his vote but with a cautious twist:
*Remember, switching from the court to classroom isn't
irreversible. Just teach a couple years, write the book on
sentencing, then return to courtroom life.*

I signed Earl's contract and we interviewed at law schools from Virginia to Hawaii. Drusilla and I settled on an independent institution set in sunny San Diego: California Western School of Law. I'd run its nascent legal clinic and pontificate behind a podium. Our cross-country move would put us in the Golden State, nearer San Francisco.

On my last day in the District of Columbia I hugged sad farewells with colleagues at Law Students in Court. Driving out of town, I circled both federal and local courthouses. Warrior wondered, *How much of your lifetime's sweat and energy did you leave inside those buildings, helping clients as you learned to practice freedom law?*

My mind was flicking through some litigation triumphs when it felt a buried question burst inside my chest: *Have you just turned your back on courtrooms and the life you'd dreamt about since you were six?*

Hell no! bellowed warrior, smacking his right fist against the dash. Freedom lawyer watched a courthouse dwindle in the rear-view mirror, then turned around and yelled, *Don't forget— Campbell's coming back!*

In July my wife and I set out on a scenic route to San Diego, steering clear of every interstate. In our latest acquisition— a non-air-conditioned Beetle— we had crammed our five-month son, two daffy Irish Setters, and a Siamese cat named Felony. After ten cramped torrid days of improv-on-the-fly, we arrived at California Western School of Law.

I soon found myself immersed in life inside a bricks-and-mortar school. Compared to restive jurors, classroom students were delights— they *paid* to sit and hear me talk!

Formal teaching also slammed me into ironies I now genially accept. To learn how law school really worked, I had to penetrate its jungle of appearances and myths. But just as I had once idealized a courtroom's hunt for truth, I'd romanticized that search inside the corridors of academe.

Liberated from the constant clutch of D.C. politics, I discovered law schools also trafficked in covert agendas, inflated egos, rank hypocrisies, and power grabs.

Even favorite colleagues brandished flowery rationales to cover machiavellian moves. It took me a while to believe the truth of William James: "Academic politics are so vicious precisely because the stakes are so small."

Drusilla once asked why I grew so jaded standing in the steady rain of law-school legerdemain: "Art, can't you admit professors are just people after all?"

I responded, "Dru, I have no problem with that view. And I acknowledge politics are part of every social structure known to man. Like toilets, they're necessities of life and can't be ignored. I've been known to use a restroom now and then. But I get tired of manipulation by the folks who spend all day in there."

At first I ducked skullduggeries by sinking into scholarship. Although never kindling passion for the subject, I spent two years writing LAW OF SENTENCING. The tome became a nationwide authority, complete with one more irony: I had to write an update every year.

Decades later, having sired three editions and a horde of yearly supplements, I likened the experience to riding on a tiger's back: There was no convenient method to dismount.

But after I'd fulfilled my plan of publishing this book, I found myself reluctant to return to litigation life. Sometimes after two martinis warrior poked me in the ribs: *Isn't this the time you said that you'd go back to court?*

"Let's discuss it later," I responded, summoning another round.

One autumn day a dozen roses landed at my door, sent by a former client from D.C. They brought fragrant jolts of victory and gratitude but also asked, *Art, have you let your dream of San Francisco solo-practice fade? Have you succumbed to living inside sheltered campus walls?* A few days later I was glad to help these flowers take up residence inside our compost bin.

For the first time as a grown-up, teaching gave me time to stroll down non-law paths of reading and reflection. But time, along with student questions, prodded me to ponder issues I'd put off for years: *Who are you really? What's your purpose? What's life all about?*

No longer could concerns of clients shield me from existential question marks like these; now they sliced me to the bone. As I'd once done with courts and academe, I had to search for truth inside *myself*.

I must probe the politics of my subconscious, ferret out the silent deals it had made that let large chunks of me be run by forces hidden from my sight.

* * * * *

That led me to unearth addiction in my life. From adolescence onward I had always wanted to achieve and to excel— in everything from music, sports, and scholarship to winning courtroom trials.

These traits weren't evil in themselves but in me they took a toxic twist: I *needed* to achieve; I was *driven* to excel. I couldn't *live* except in constant motion, fearing silence, shunning immobility. At night I couldn't fall asleep unless I first checked off a list of my accomplishments.

Every project must be done on time and perfectly. If competing with another— I'd invent a rival if there wasn't one— my work must be superior. Warrior, spurred on by adrenalin, reveled in this way of life.

Now, as I began to shoulder more self-honesty, I realized my endless search for conquests didn't come from my free will. I seemed powerless to keep from taking on new tasks and finishing them obsessively. I was addicted to activity.

How to grapple with this baffling malady? I sought support from others like myself. Starting San Diego's chapter of Workaholics Anonymous, I later helped launch W.A.'s World Service Organization.

Meeting every week with fellow addicts gave me fortitude and insight. Our collective courage helped us realize we ran to phantom arms that held out promises of status and self-worth if only we engaged in ceaseless work.

Our culture worships this chimera. It slathers guarantees of money, power, and prestige as it devours true believers' lives, alchemizing human beings to human doings. Tragically, practitioners display their workaholic yokes with pride or treat this life-devouring syndrome as a joke.

My activity addition also led me to discover what my warrior dined upon: Fear. Of course, hard-wired inside every human's DNA is prehistoric dread of yawning sabre-tooths. But Scottish Highland genes and a dysfunctional childhood nurtured mine beyond the norm.

In courtrooms warrior had been constantly on guard for any fact or witness that could leap out, botch my evidence, stunt my strategy, foil my argument, lock my client in a cage, or make me look the fool. It wasn't hard for me to see how fear kept warrior vigilant in court.

But outside court denial cloaked the subtle ways fear ran my life, while machismo tried to hide my apprehension from the world. Eventually I found the guts to see how large a role it played.

Skulking just beneath my consciousness, fear reared whenever it perceived a threat from anyone or anything. To be expected in a sport or heated argument, fear also rose in sundry social scenes. In order to be free, I had to track this dragon to its lair.

Spelunking caves of my unconscious, I was humbled to discover how plebian was my beast. It was fear of the unknown: concern that I could not control all unfamiliar incidents.

Since my self-image and beliefs staked out the familiar, anything that menaced them could kick my fear awake. Once aroused, it ordered warrior to locate an enemy and hack away until I felt in charge.

Fueled by rushes of adrenalin, fighter always focused on external foes and never peered inside. Every conquest temporarily eased my need for managing— until another threat arose.

After years of shooting daily fixes of adrenalin— with my workaholic's rationale to justify it all— I'd become a full-fledged junkie.

Compared to substance-addicts in recovery, I was double taxed: I had to cope with my addiction to the workaholic *process* plus my *drug* of choice.

One day at a law-school gathering, warrior nearly leapt across the table to defend what felt like an attack on my self-image. When we came home I steered fighter to a mirror like the one that Alice dreamed in WONDERLAND.

We found the giant caterpillar curled on a toadstool, puffing on his water pipe. He stared at us a moment, then blew rings of smoke that framed the classic query, *Who... Are... You...?*

I'd been haunted by this figure since I was a kid and watched Walt Disney's film of Lewis Carroll's book. His question stalked me through my adolescence and four troubled Harvard years.

The caterpillar's challenge only ceased when I placed all my chips upon a trial-law career. Then I could boldly wave at any passing mirror, "Hi, there— I'm a freedom lawyer."

But the more I settled into academe, the dimmer this self-image grew. Attending law-school graduations, watching students march down roads of destiny, freedom lawyer offered muffled maybe's to my edgy soul: *Maybe next year you'll return to court; maybe then you'll regain your identity.*

Leisure in my pocket carried further hazards to my former sense of self. Other roles grew brighter: teacher, counselor, ex-musician, husband, father, friend.

One day I paused before two facing mirrors at a gym. Suddenly I heard the caterpillar's mocking voice. This time he tossed a different taunt: *Will the real Campbell please step forth?*

Fear stuck me with its hypodermic. With mirrors on both sides, I was sandwiched by an endless row of opposites: freedom lawyer versus warrior; litigator versus teacher; poet versus academic; feeler versus reasoner; dreamer versus doer; jock v. scholar; polemicist v. ponderer.

No longer could I duck these warring contradictions; for years they had been feuding in my gut. Caterpillar was now charging me with harboring hypocrisies.

Fear dispatched my warrior to subdue all inconsistencies. Some days he boosted his adrenalin with alcohol and other drugs. But no matter what he tried, fighter never vanquished either one of an opposing pair.

Zen finally shattered all these mind-forged manacles. From pre-law days I'd zazened intermittently, glimpsing how my mind played tricks to block me from perceiving and experiencing reality.

Nonetheless for decades I had summoned warrior to effectuate my lifetime strategy: *Control all outer changes and be safe; control all inner conflicts and be whole.*

Now, as I dove deeper into Zen, I saw life was constant change. Trying to control its fabulous complexity was not only futile but prolonged my warrior's slavery to fear. What if I ceased attempts to manage new events? What if I simply looked at and experienced them instead?

Each time warrior dropped his sword, I felt a surge of peace and energy. Finally right-side up in life, I began investigating how conditioned thoughts had nurtured fear, intensified my restlessness, blurred my eyesight, and consumed my time.

Looking back, I saw I'd blended workaholism, fear, and conquest into a compelling trinity. From their throne in my unconscious they had ruled me with the power of an unexamined god.

Returning to the gym, I stepped again between the two-faced looking glass, then glanced left and right. Eureka— suddenly I saw my images and their mirrored opposites were totally self-made!

I had pasted polar labels on each one and dressed them in contrasting clothes. From early childhood my subconscious had included and excluded certain traits, then joined them with selected actions to create "the story of me."

Conveniently revised from time to time, that story had become my "self" and, when acting in the world, was my self-image, my identity.

Yet what society had posed as contradictions— even freedom lawyer versus warrior— were just yin-yang aspects of my real self. My core was not corralled by shifting slats of words.

Fortified with this new insight, I found a solitary looking glass. Beckoning the caterpillar, I dared him to repeat his smoke-signed *Who Are You*. When he did I smiled, thrust one finger in his cursive haze, traced a circle, and replied, "Awareness, Sir."

Freed from cultural conventions that would split the world and me into arrays of dueling pairs, I could tango down grand corridors of life that used to look like hopeless hostile labyrinths.

I still saluted flags of freedom law. They remained my guide in legal matters but no longer blanketed my world. Freedom lawyer was a part of me, but not my totality.

Zen held the key each time I felt locked in boxes of conditioned thought. I discovered the most potent cartons were created from intangibles— abstractions milled by brains compelled to cram life into categories.

Likewise law— but happily not justice— had been stuffed in classified containers. For example, contracts must be subdivided into offer, acceptance, consideration, etc. Sides of boxes often stunted lawyers' views of life that lay outside.

Do you know an occupational hazard of law profs? We "solve problems" by writing unread articles that merely re-arrange or re-form legal categories.

So I finally realized my fears of non-control or contradiction needn't block my genuine response to life or cripple my relationships. With old courage but new insight I began to greet the real world— embracing both its pains and ecstasies.

I looked up a former lover: poetry. I'd lived with her before the law— that jealous mistress— made me swear unrivaled fealty. Edmund Burke was right about law's sharpening the mind by narrowing it.

Glad to high-five my abandoned muse and frolic through unbounded worlds, I returned to reading, writing, publishing, and meeting other poets to discuss our work.

* * * * *

Warrior got a special gift from Zen. Although life was steady change, he realized that didn't make it constant war. Now he could *choose* the knolls on which to make his stand. One day he tugged my sleeve: "_Between our wisely chosen battles, Art, what's left for me to do? I'm bored._"

I said, "How's this for a challenge?" and explained that in a month would come the San Diego Marathon. Warrior once had been a sprinter; now he sometimes jogged for fun but never rambled longer than ten miles. Would he like to try for twenty-six? *Sure!* he said— and did.

So warrior found a way to deal with his hunger for adrenalin. For years he powered me through distance races: 5Ks, 10Ks, marathons, triathlons, etcetera. His favorite mental game? Transforming them to competitions in which beating prior times or slower runners was his test to do or die.

* * * * *

Freedom lawyer also found a new reward. One day, prepping for a class, I glanced back at litigation days. I saw opposing lawyers as directors of two rival films, each performing their own edits of the actors' testimony and spotlighting certain props.

They jostled for acceptance by a judge or jury of their version of disputed incidents. Although focused on one level of a multilayered scene, each director claimed his screen portrayed the one and only "truth."

From this reverie it struck me that a law-school class might use a multifacet view. While I projected cases through the lens of law and legal-think, I could sometimes also place them inside freedom-lawyer frames. The latter would reveal win-win outcomes for all parties— even those affected but not listed in the case.

As students mastered rules and rationales, they'd also see that freedom-lawyer values— fairness, justice for the powerless, respect for all concerned— could be pursued in any legal specialty.

I changed from wearing suits and jackets to what felt more natural: jeans and running shoes. In part I honored student expectations, also donning dress shirts and a tie. With this sartorial quarrel as my graphic yin and yang, I strode to class with rehabilitated zeal.

Not only could I reach beyond twelve jurors in a trial, I was
touching those who'd practice after I'd been boxed as ashes
in a columbarium.

Inviting students to consider freedom-law as a career, each
year I was pleased to see a few accept. Now when I
perused the daily news, instead of feeling guilt or longing,
I rejoiced at other freedom lawyers' feats.

Sometimes warrior's charger trotted to my side and
whinnied for a ride. Stroking witches' stirrups from his
tangled mane, I cupped his ear and told him we had both
grown old: "Now's the time when teachers teach and
writers write. Let younger fighters fight."

Then came the day my wife Drusilla was arrested.

CALIFORNIA VERSUS CAMPBELL

I: PROTEST

Our lives begin to end the day we become silent about things that matter. — Martin Luther King, Jr.

On a chilly autumn morning thirty San Diegans gathered at an unfenced parking lot. Like a harmless apron, asphalt stretched around five unpretentious buildings. Inside purred a nuclear-weapons plant.

A major Pentagon contractor ran the factory. Its workers fashioned Tomahawks— not low-tech weapons made to smash combatants face-to-face— these were guided missiles made to hurl devastation across an ocean or a continent.

For weeks this group of citizens had picketed one border of the twenty-acre parking lot, handing leaflets to employees as 5000 daily workers came and left the factory. Some handouts claimed the plant made San Diego the prime target for a Soviet nuclear attack.

Other sheets reminded workers that their toil violated international law. Some leaflets urged, "Why not convert your skills to making products that promote world peace?"

These San Diegans weren't alone. Over six-hundred other protest groups had sprung up in the U.S.A., all objecting to the unchecked growth of nuclear arms.

At the time a law-review observed what many folks and history-writers now forget: "The amount and extent of nonviolent civil resistance activities in America during the 1980s dwarfed the occasionally violent anti-Vietnam War demonstrations of the 1960s."

What started as our nation's race to build defensive weapons had evolved into a mindless fiend; our country had stockpiled missiles to destroy the planet's population many times.

Fully armed, each tomahawk's throw-weight landing in an urban center would destroy ten-thousand souls; other nearby thousands would be doomed to radiation death.

Officially the U.S. strategy was called Mutual Assured Destruction (note the aptness of this acronym): If Soviets dared strike our land with nuclear weaponry, we'd retaliate with overwhelming missiles and annihilate their populace.

The ultimate result was not a secret but seldom mentioned in the mainstream press: In a full-scale exchange, total detonations would prompt nuclear winter, eventually destroying every human on the planet.

A syndicated cartoon caught the global zeitgeist: Presidents Gorbachev and Reagan stood *mano a mano,* flicking lighted matches at each other. Idea bubbles from their heads showed each leader hoped his counterpart would be first to flinch. What made the silly image solemn was the context: Both men stood inside a spreading pool of gasoline.

When picketing and leaflets didn't halt what demonstrators feared would be a lock-step march to Armageddon, the San Diegans felt they had to chart another course.

Older members remembered days of "duck and cover," when school children were assured they could survive atomic blasts by crouching underneath their desks.

Other folks had watched or marched in 1960s protests against sex and race discrimination. Arrests of demonstrators had sparked widespread coverage in the news, kindled public consciousness, and ultimately transformed our country's laws.

Still other members of the group had proudly fought in Vietnam. They now joined ranks of former anti-war protestors, whose mass arrests and trials had caused another turn-around in public policy.

At an organizational meeting the leafleteers aired varied views of what more they should do. After many hours they arrived at a consensus: Unite with other protesters in this country and the world.

They'd be San Diego's representatives in what would be a National Day of Disarmament, part of demonstrations round the world in an International Week of Action.

First they wrote a formal letter to officials at the plant, pointing out the factory's role in placing both their city and humanity at risk. They urged the factory switch its expertise to making tools of peace.

Group leaders told news media of their plan to march across the factory's parking lot so they could hand their letter to officials at the plant.

Some members planned to occupy a 60-foot-wide strip across one edge of the lot. If arrested, they hoped the publicity would alert San Diegans to the madness driving current U.S. policy. To ensure their acts stayed peaceful, demonstrators held a workshop on non-violence

On the designated day thirty members walked along the tarmac's edge. When police arrived and warned them they were trespassers, twenty-one refused to leave or show I.D. Instead they sat down on the blacktop.

The group had previously agreed they'd not go limp upon arrest; that could set off use of force and mar their mission of promoting peace. Police politely helped them to their feet, bound their wrists with plastic ties, and carted them to jail.

II: PARTICIPANTS

Universal history is an infinite sacred book
that all men write and read and try to understand,
and in which they too are written. — Thomas Carlyle

The demonstrators' demographics were an ad-man's dream. Their ranks included teachers, two grandparents, Girl Scout leader, minister, Catholic nun, hard-hat worker, pregnant mother, ex-probation officer, and a novelist. The latter was my wife, Drusilla. Her name eventually became the title of my final trial.

San Diego's City Attorney lodged a single charge of trespass against each demonstrator. Guilt could dock a convict's bank account $500 and change her daily outlook to six months of grey-bar days.

For weeks before the group's arrest, I was not involved. Although I backed my wife's endeavors, I'd joined a global group of lawyers invoking international law to halt the suicidal race for nuclear supremacy.

When arrestees bickered over choosing guilty pleas or trials, Dru suggested specialized advice. Next time they met I tagged along. Eventually they chose me their pro-bono representative.

Thus began the toughest string of client conferences in my career. First, there wasn't just one person with a single outlook on the case. Instead a score of souls sought inconsistent goals from diverse points of view.

From this emerged a time-consuming precept of the group. Before accepting my advice on any strategy or tactic, demonstrators would debate until they reached consensus:

"We've always made *collective* choices where and when and how to stop nuclear war. We must likewise honor this procedure for all issues in the court." Thus endless squabbles over minor matters became bound to group integrity.

Another challenge came from some protestors' natural mistrust of attorneys. I was part of "the establishment," the very types who threatened conflagration of the world. Two other lawyers also volunteered their services. However their participation often knotted up analysis; my advice became just one of three.

Cullen Beardwood was a recent law-school graduate who was billed "the people's lawyer." Handsome, in his twenties with a flowing ponytail, he looked clearly counter-culture. I'm not sure I ever banished his suspicion of that balding academic who'd once practiced as a "fed" in Washington, D.C.

The other attorney was Bezelle Chatsworth, a burly former firefighter, now self-styled "lawyer for the poor." Also twenty-something, he'd returned to San Diego to share what he had learned from helping other protest groups.

At first the demonstrators thought it more strategic to appear in court without a lawyer. Each one would demand a separate trial, hoping for the chance to spread their doomsday warnings to as many juries as they could.

Splinter members of our group— non-clients who'd been charged with trespass at a prior time and place— decided to pursue this strategy. Months later one of them unwittingly would nearly sink our case.

Another two or three who'd been arrested with my wife felt honor-bound to accept blame for their civil disobedience. They declined my services and pled guilty or no-contest to the trespass charge.

After hours of tortuous debate, the remainder of the group finally wrestled one consensus to the ground: They'd create the greatest impact on the public's consciousness by combining all their cases in a single trial with yours truly as chief counsel.

However, that decision sprung Pandora's Box. Lawyer codes assert that clients only get to make three choices— go to trial, have a jury, and sit in the witness chair. Beyond these, strategies and tactics should reside in lawyers' hands.

Not so with these clients. They made clear that representing them was on condition that *all* aspects of the case be cranked through their protracted grinder of consensus.

Before we stepped inside a court, we spent scores of hours haggling over pre-trial motions, juror preferences, court attire, statements to the press, et incessant cetera.

Strong-willed clients pressed their private views of how a trial *ought* to be. Their notions rose from dreams and media portrayals untempered by reality. They seemed convinced that real law eats children in their sleep.

After days of painstaking diplomacy the other two
attorneys and I finally brokered courtroom strategies that
still promoted anti-missile aspirations of our clientele.

Later during trial, consensus rituals gulped down large
amounts of time. When on my feet I'd catch a signal from
one client and ask the judge for "just a moment to confer."
What followed were extended parleys with three rows of
co-defendants leaning forward in their seats.

I valued and respected every client individually, but
collectively they helter-skeltered like a mob of mules on
rollerskates. Visualize a veteran sergeant in the midst of
combat, having to discuss his plan with each novice soldier
before countering an adversary's move. Nothing in my
military, sports, or courtroom background had prepared
me for this task.

At trial's end Chatsworth sidled up to me. "Campbell, you
should write a lawyer's handbook on the endless
problems— and the cures we improvised— in representing
a collective group of protest clients."

If I ever wrote that book, its refrain would echo Winston
Churchill's message to commencement graduates: "Never
give up— never, never, never, never, never."

III: JUDGES

The curse of the elective system
is it turns almost every judge into a politician.
— Henry T. Lummus

Know what freaks out judges? Jury trials without lawyers.
Judges know defendants have a constitutional right to
represent themselves. But black robers hurl dire warnings
at a lawyer-less defendant to dissuade her from that right.
"Ma'am, you've heard the adage 'One who represents
herself has a fool for a client?' Well, those words are
very true."

120

It's judicial agony to try to shield jurors from all prejudicial statements or improper evidence that's loosed by litigants not bludgeoned into proper protocol by years of schooling in the law.

I seized this specter as my pre-trial ace. Did San Diego jurists want the grief of nineteen separate jury trials, each spearheaded by an amateur? Moreover, these particular defendants might elevate their anti-missile message over their regard for courtroom etiquette or fear of sanctions for contempt.

I arranged to meet with the presiding judge of Muni Court to discuss my clients' pending trials. The Honorable Constance Witherball was a stickler for efficiency. I knew she wouldn't relish large expenditures of personnel and time for what the press had ballyhooed the "city's largest-ever group of protest trials."

Outside the judge's chambers I met my learned opposition. Deputy City Attorney introduced himself as Richard Shaw. I shook his hand and said, "Please, call me Art. Can I refer to you as Rick?" He rolled his eyes and said, "Might as well—everybody does. Can't seem to shake that image of an Asian taxicab."

In his late forties, standing five-feet eight, Rick Shaw cut a handsome figure in his dark-brown suit. Word was he loved to litigate. But I knew he couldn't try all nineteen cases by himself; so his office would be sorely strapped for trial lawyers.

The judge's clerk invited Shaw and me inside her honor's inner-sanctum. We introduced ourselves and shook hands with Judge Witherball. After sharing comments on the weather but declining soft drinks, tea, and coffee, Shaw and I were gestured toward deep leather chairs.

Witherball stepped behind a massive walnut desk; from her elevated swivel-chair she looked down at us. "Gentlemen, my clerk's informed me of your pending protest cases. Is there anything the court can do for you in this regard?"

Sounding casual, I brought up my clients' early preference to maintain the status quo: separate trials without counsel. "But instead of taking all that courthouse time, they've agreed to let the court consolidate their cases to a single trial and have me represent them all."

Judge Witherball let out her breath and leaned back in her chair. "However," I continued, "they said they'd do it only on condition." I paused as Witherball and Shaw sat up, their smiles disappearing quick as chipmunks. The judge asked sternly, "And what's that, Mr. Campbell?"

"That I select our trial judge," I said politely and relaxed inside my wing-backed chair.

Judge Witherball turned a laser gaze at Shaw. "That seems reasonable to me. Any objection from the City Attorney's office?"

For five seconds Shaw stared at the Persian carpet, waiting for an answer to appear. One did: "It's only right that our side have the chance to approve or disapprove of Mr. Campbell's choice."

Nearly free of one potential migraine, the jurist focused her determined look on me. "Well, Mr. Campbell, doesn't that sound fair to you?"

"Sounds good theoretically. If things don't work out, your honor, can the two of us come back to you?"

"I hope that won't be necessary," she said severely, rising from her chair to indicate our tête á tête was done.

It took another evening's colloquy for clients to agree with my criteria for a jurist in this case. To deal with some touchy topics in our multi-layered defense, our judge must be uncommonly intelligent, long-suffering, and apolitical.

From talks with local lawyers I believed Judge Dudley Cuttles fit this bill. I'd known him casually before he had ascended to the bench. In his fifties, Cuttles had a tall and

gangly frame, his tonsure picketed by blonde unruly hair.
He was exceptionally intelligent.

Since he'd been a liberal lawyer, I hoped he'd have the
wherewithal to comprehend our points of view about the
case's controversial issues and contentious evidence.

However, Rick Shaw knew him as a working judge. So I
was instantly suspicious when the prosecutor told me he
had no objection to my choice.

IV: PRETRIAL MOTIONS

*I do not know how the Third World War will be fought
but I can tell you what they will use in the Fourth— rocks!*
— Albert Einstein

To help juries focus on the proper evidence, pretrial
motions try to clear away all major issues not for jurors'
eyes. In this trial we planned launching unconventional
defenses. Of course, Rick Shaw aimed to shoot them down.
Pretrial hearings would let Cuttles rule which could fly
above the jury box.

Before drafting any motions I conferred with dozens of
attorneys. Obtaining the addresses of over 600 groups of
citizens protesting nuclear arms across the U.S.A., I
contacted twenty-eight.

My consultation catalog included fifteen San Diego lawyers
and another twenty-four in California and beyond. My heart
danced a rumba when letters from some freedom lawyers
greeted me with "Welcome back."

* * * * *

Our first motion sought to raise the "Nuremberg Defense,"
from a concept born at Allied trials in Japan and Germany
right after World War II.

One legal scholar summarized its premise: "Anyone with knowledge of illegal activity and an opportunity to do something about it is a potential criminal under international law unless the person takes affirmative measures to prevent commission of the crimes."

But three towering barricades stood directly in our path. To scale them with normal ladders would require huge amounts of cash. First we'd have to prove official U.S. policy aimed our country's arsenal of missiles at civilians, schools, hospitals, and non-combatant homes.

Next we'd have to show this action was illegal under treaties the U.S. had signed. Finally we would have to demonstrate the state of California recognized these treaties as its "law."

The standard way to prove these propositions was to fly in well known experts; they'd tack down each point with testimony from the witness chair. Since my clients couldn't foot a smidgen of this cost, our first motion listed cases that said justice shouldn't rest upon the size of a defendant's purse.

That motion also urged our judge to open up his mind: "In order to make judicial rulings in this case, the Court is asked to engage in the unusual effort of thinking of world annihilation in legal terms."

We appended public documents supporting all our points. Among papers proving that our nation's military strategy meant killing non-combatants was a congressional report.

This account concluded that "a limited or 'counter-force' attack' of nuclear weapons would kill up to twenty-million people immediately and cause millions more cancer deaths and genetic defects. An all-out attack on a range of military and economic targets using a large fraction of the existing nuclear arsenal would cause up to 160 million immediate deaths...."

On the issue of legality, no less than eight U.N. resolutions in the preceding quarter-century had condemned creation of nuclear bombs and insisted on cessation of the race to build and stockpile missiles to deliver them.

We attached more than a dozen treaties, charters, resolutions, and conventions, each of which our country had endorsed. I summarized their bottom line: "They prohibit weapons that aggravate suffering, kill noncombatants, destroy nonmilitary structures, employ poisonous substances, eradicate plant or animal species, or cause genocide."

Instead of calling experts to the witness chair, we requested that Judge Cuttles take "judicial notice of the facts" presented in these documents. Then, under the Constitution's Supremacy Clause, I argued all signed treaties were a part of California law.

We were elated when the judge ruled every fact and treaty was legitimate. *What a break! Now we can expose our jurors and the public to this crucial information— always downplayed by the White House and compliant media.*

Then the judge blindsided me. He snatched a book on civil disobedience and pointed to its central argument: "Nuremberg defendants must demonstrate a moral choice was forced upon them *by the law they disobeyed.*"

Although I hadn't mentioned this peculiar tome, Cuttles chomped its pages as a horse would sweetened oats. They let him masticate a killer syllogism:

Premise-one: My clients were accused of trespass, a crime that forced no moral choice on them. Premise-two: Defendants had no duty to resist the crime of trespass under international law. Conclusion: The accused possessed no Nuremberg defense.

Cuttles dragged in a non-sequitur to buttress his imperative: Defendants showed "no immediate direct harm to themselves... that is different from the potential harm that might affect every other person in the United States."

As a final kick the jurist ruled our defense raised "political questions" which lay in the exclusive province of Congress and the President.

Both warrior and my freedom lawyer howled: *What's going on?! The judge just ruled our facts and law were true. Why go so far afield to conclude they don't state a defense?*

At the time I didn't realize the power of hot-button politics to block logic in a court. Had I been more aware, it would have made what followed easier to take. As we marched on with other pretrial motions, I watched each soldier of the rational disappear inside the black hole of a standard jurist's robe.

* * * * *

Our second motion raised the defense of "necessity," an ancient but still extant Anglo Saxon rule that justified a detrimental act in order to prevent a greater harm. If my clients trespassed on an unfenced parking lot, they were justified because they did so to protect the human race.

Of course we had to show the judge that we had evidence to satisfy this rule— then jurors would determine if our evidence was true.

We relied on the same documents Cuttles had accepted earlier, adding other writings by acknowledged experts in their field. Collectively they showed our country's planned retaliation under M.A.D. would leave a billion casualties and trigger global winter that eventually would snuff out life on earth.

Once more Cuttles took judicial notice of our facts, but this time used judicial judo to hold they did not amount to a legitimate defense. Although the doctrine of necessity was deeply rooted in our nation's law, a minor court in California once sub-divided it into six elements. Judge Cuttles ruled we had to satisfy each one.

I'll skip the elements we met. According to the judge, our proof fell short on three. First we hadn't shown that escalating threats between our country and the Soviets, backed by bulging missile silos, made exchange of deadly missiles "imminent."

Why not? Pointing to a fact beside the point, the learned judge asserted, "The possibility of nuclear annihilation has existed for several years."

Next he said we hadn't shown that other ways to lessen threats of war were "unavailable." Finally, we had not convinced him that the means defendants chose were "reasonable."

On this last point I argued vigorously: "Surely, judge, you realize how many times this country's history has been shaped from protests by its citizens. Many scholars place this nation's birth— indeed its conception— on a media event its leaders dubbed the Boston Tea Party."

I added, "In the last two decades, public demonstrations triggered nationwide reforms in race and gender when our legislatures and executives lost their moral compasses. So surely it was 'reasonable' to think one way to save the earth was to join a worldwide protest that would focus people's minds upon our planet's plight."

I finished with a fundamental point: "Regardless how your *honor* views our nation's history or my clients' acts, 'reasonableness' is a question of *fact*. And, of course, there's no more basic rule than it's the province of a *jury* to decide the facts."

Nonetheless, the judge held reasonableness so clearly nonexistent that for jurors to decide that it was there would rest on speculation— a process that's taboo. "Counselor, the court denies your defense of necessity."

Warrior mused sardonically: *Sorry, Judge, I can't agree. Even if I did, we'd both be wrong.*

* * * * *

One fruitful product lodged inside the tangle of these
arguments. Richard Shaw plucked out a phrase that
formed fresh notions in my mind. As I argued that
"necessity" should justify attempts to stop the missile plant,
Shaw quipped, "Sounds like Mr. Campbell's arguing crime-
prevention here."

'Zounds, said freedom lawyer, *that could be a new defense!*
I've never heard of crime-prevention in the context of these
facts. It means my clients had a right to stop the missile
plant from breaking international law.

Although the rationale of this defense was like necessity's—
justifying lesser evils if they stopped a greater one— this
concept covered situations where the greater evil was
a *crime*.

At our next recess I slipped away and strolled the
courthouse halls alone. I had to wrap my mind around
Shaw's casual but intriguing idea.

Freedom lawyer mused: *The groundwork's all been laid for*
this defense. Cuttles took judicial notice of everything we'll
need. He okayed the treaties and accepted our position
that they're part of California law. That means he's agreed
with our conclusion that just planning missile strikes to kill
non-combatants is a "crime."

This and other treaty violations were precisely what my
clients tried to stop. But how do I persuade his honor that
a crime-prevention defense differs from "necessity?"

I returned to court and asked the judge to recess for the
balance of the day so I could research this new point. "No
problem from this side," chirped Shaw. "I'd like time to
check it out myself."

That evening Cuttles also burned some midnight oil. Next
day in court the judge slammed me into the same wall he'd
built to block our defense of necessity.

"Mr. Campbell, under crime-prevention your clients still must have acted 'reasonably'."

"Your honor, what could be *more* reasonable than sitting on a parking lot to stop a crime that could destroy the earth?"

Cuttles answered, "I have no problem saying which acts are the *greater* crime. But can you convince this court that danger to the earth is more than theoretical?"

I responded, "Since invention of the crossbow, when has the latest weapon not been used? Did we drop atomic bombs on Japan by accident? In a nuclear strike is it likely either we or Russia would surrender while a single general or admiral still held missiles to destroy the enemy?"

"Counselor, I'm still troubled by the *means* your clients chose. They tried to change official policy by coverage in the press. Show me how that's reasonable, especially when a nuclear strike's not imminent."

"Judge, first of all the law's *already* being broken by our country's *planning* mutually assured destruction. That's one crime my clients tried to stop with time-tested means that redirected policies in civil rights and Vietnam."

Since Cuttles didn't interrupt, I said, "Looking at the imminence of war, how much warning of a Soviet missile launch would our country get? According to the articles under your judicial notice, at most our nation would have thirty minutes. If my clients waited for the wail of a civil-defense siren, they'd be far too late. The only reasonable way to stop a launch and counter-launch was to act *before* that time."

I ended with a question I believed compelled a Yes: "What can be more reasonable in a news-dependent nation than informing citizens about an industry that not only threatens to annihilate humanity but acts in daily violation of the law?"

As Rick Shaw rose to argue, the judge extended his right arm, palm-down. "Since I ruled previously— under the necessity defense— that defendants' means weren't reasonable, I'll be consistent and rule the same way now. Mr. Campbell, you may not present a crime-prevention defense."

Freedom lawyer tried to cover warrior's look of shock: *This could be a major issue on appeal.* "Your honor, just to make our record clear, are you holding as a matter of law no rational juror could find my clients' actions reasonable?"

"That's right, counselor."

Freedom lawyer sat down staring at my notes in disbelief: *Why won't Cuttles follow logic in this case? Does he fear a jury might agree it's reasonable to protest the way my clients did? Is he scared this case might clear the way for crackpot groups to orchestrate a trespass so they too can get their issues in the news?*

But warrior's thoughts descended to a darker place: *Has Cuttles lost his legal testicles? Have black robes dyed his heart conservative and his brain political? Is he afraid to be the first judge in the country to trust jurors with these issues? Is he frightened he'll be branded "liberal" or "activist"? Does he fear for his career?*

* * * * *

Years of hindsight have convinced me Cuttles acted like a normal trial judge. Most black-robers quake at what might happen if the logic of necessity and crime-prevention were extended to protect contentious acts of politics.

Ordinary jurists cling to their judicial branch and chirp that any switch in public policy must sprout from other branches of our government— and never bloom from acts of those accused of crime.

But, as Sartre once observed, "Not to decide is to decide." Cuttles' snub of our defenses was still an exercise of politics; it upheld the status quo. Since warrior's eyes could only see the logic of our arguments, when Cuttles swept them all aside, I felt cut off at the knees.

This ruling also marked the moment that my clients— expecting they at least would get to tell a jury *why* they'd acted as they did— lost their trust in Cuttles, courtrooms, law, and me.

* * * * *

We had a fourth pretrial motion. I argued for the right to show our jurors that defendants acted without criminal intent. I summarized it orally: "Your honor, California's trespass statute says, for defendants to be guilty, they must have acted 'willfully,' i.e., with criminal intent. If not, their acts were innocent."

In fairness to Judge Cuttles, he correctly speared this argument. With Rick Shaw's prompting, he asserted in this context "willfully" didn't mean defendants had an "evil" mind. To violate the statute, they merely had to "know what they were doing and act from their own wills."

* * * * *

After these pretrial motions were denied, co-counsel Cullen Beardwood was incensed. But like a good attorney he funneled his frustrations through a vessel of the law. He believed defendants' protest was protected by the First Amendment: Our clients had a constitutional right to publicize their politics.

I didn't think case-law supported us. The fatal fact was that our clients had proclaimed their views on private property during business hours when other times and places were available.

But freedom lawyer honored Cullen's passion, so I stood aside and let him champion this position. He made a valiant argument that First Amendment principles should trump a charge of trespassing. But Cuttles— citing contra California cases— shot him down.

* * * * *

A few days prior to our trial this is where we stood. Judge
Cuttles ruled we couldn't mount an international-law
defense. Nor could we demonstrate necessity or prove
prevention of what might be mankind's final crime. He
stiff-armed claims protestors lacked criminal intent and
wouldn't drop the trespass charge on First Amendment
grounds.

Often when defenseless, one's best strategy is seizing the
offensive. We decided to attack the weakest part of Rick
Shaw's case. In order to convict for trespass, he must
prove the parking lot was closed to members of the public.
At that point I now focused all my energy.

V: TRIAL STRATEGY

Not preparing for battle is the greatest of crimes.
To be prepared for any contingency
is the greatest of virtues.
— Sun Tzu

We launched a three-pronged thrust against the
prosecutor's case. He had to prove the missile factory's
parking lot was not open to the public. We aimed to
destroy this claim.

First we fired a *subpoena duces tecum* at the missile plant.
Essentially it said "under punishment of law, you're ordered
to bring listed things with you to court."

We served it on the chief security officer, demanding "every
document that mentions policies about the private nature
of, or public access to, the parking lot surrounding your
facility."

Feathers hit the fan. I had no doubt the factory's brass had
prodded Shaw to beat down our command. He brought

132

predicted arguments to render our subpoena void. First, he claimed disclosure of such texts would compromise the safety of a weapons factory— i.e., endanger national security.

Next he pointed out that no one in the case— not even Cuttles— should lay eyes upon these documents unless that person held a national security clearance.

One might guess defendants didn't have such clearances. Neither did the judge or prosecutor. Ironically I'd garnered two in my career: one from days I'd been an Air Force navigator, another as a Special Assistant U.S. Attorney for the District of Columbia.

I made a solemn pledge that I'd prevent the public or my clients from learning any military secrets I unearthed from the documents. I offered to examine them inside a room without a window and let missile-factory guards with pistols loom above my chair.

But since neither judge nor prosecutor was cleared to see what I could see, the adversary system wouldn't let just one side of a trial paw through secret documents. Cuttles duly quashed our subpoena.

The second prong of our defense sought to prove the parking lot was *open* to the public; thus my clients could not legally be trespassers. Our first supporting evidence surfaced on a sea of serendipity.

For years my wife and I had dined inside a steakhouse kitty-corner to the missile plant. A few nights before the trial we ate there, sharing facts of Dru's arrest with our favorite waitress, Eva Gladenstair. When I mentioned our strategic focus on the status of the parking lot, Eva raised her hands in disbelief.

"What?!" she cried. "Who says it's not open to the public? We throw after-hour parties on that tarmac nearly every Friday night. Cooks, food-handlers, bus-persons drive their cars and pick-ups on it, park, and set out picnic chairs. We

drink beer and sodas, laugh and snack and hang out—
sometimes way past midnight."

"Eva, that's terrific news!" I said. "Will you bring those facts
to court for us? Are you okay with testifying?"

"Sure," she said. "Plus there's more that you should know.
Some Saturdays I've seen Scout troop buses drive along
that lot and load up kids and gear.   Kids' parents also bring
their vans. And nearly every weekend I see guys park their
trucks and cars upon the blacktop, changing oil or
tinkering under the hood."

"That's very useful evidence, Eva," I said. "It could have a
real impact on this trial."

"Well, it's just the truth. I'm sure other workers from the
restaurant will come to court as well. They'll testify because
they like you and Dru— plus what your group is doing for
us all."

Our third prong was an experiment. As news of the
approaching trial became a subject of local— sometimes
national— media, staff and students at my law school
volunteered to help.

In response I asked if they'd feel comfortable driving their
cars to the plant during business hours. Would they see if
they're allowed to park beside the plant's reception office?

"If you're not told to leave, would you— as members of the
public— walk inside and see if anybody wants to tell you
what is going on?"

Half a dozen people eagerly agreed. They returned,
reporting they were totally ignored by plant security.
Most were handed propaganda pamphlets by front-desk
personnel. Armed with all this evidence we were set for
trial.

VI: JURORS

The tendency of the law must always be to narrow the field of uncertainty.— Justice Oliver Wendell Holmes, Jr.

Courts tweak their search for jurors as they often seine their search for truth. Unlike popular beliefs, neither party in a trial wants impartial jurors. Each side seeks a person predisposed to view the world its way.

Prospective jurors swear to speak the truth— voir dire— as attorneys pepper them with questions on their preferences and backgrounds. Answers "narrow the field of uncertainty" for each adversary.

In this case I'd ask a jury candidate, "Mr. Davidson, do you believe in gun control— would you share your thoughts with us?" Likewise Shaw would say, "Ms. Wright, have you ever been a member of a union— and if so did you ever demonstrate or go on strike?"

As voir-dire lawyers search for clues which way a candidate may lean, their questions also try to trim uncertainty by creating good impressions of the advocate, the client, and the case.

Shaw would ask, "Do you think I'm the bad guy here, someone trying to start a nuclear war or trying to prove these defendants are saboteurs or spies?"

When it came my turn, I'd say, "Do you think it's proper for leaders in our community— say, a minister or Girl Scout leader— to try to stop a war that could wipe out our planet?"

Still another way to slim uncertainty— at least when this case was tried— was to nudge potential jurors toward the lawyer's side by posing arguments and evidence as hypotheticals.

In this case my questions were directed to a single juror candidate. But I knew another fifty in the courtroom would be pondering my words:

Q. If someone walked up your driveway to hand you a letter, would you refuse to take it and instead have them arrested?

Q. Do you agree that in America citizens should have the right to exercise free speech?

Likewise Rick Shaw flung some zingers:

Q. Do you believe property always has to be fenced-in to be called 'private'?

Q. Do you believe that, notwithstanding their political beliefs, Americans should obey the law?

One can curse or marvel at this paradox: Voir dire's official rationale was exposing hidden prejudice that might taint a juror's judgment. But lawyers' queries often aimed to prejudice the jury towards the asker's side.

Shaw and I took turns firing scores of questions until our imaginations— and would-be jurors' patience— were exhausted. The process swallowed up a day and a half of courtroom time.

Twice I troubled my co-counsel by pursuing answers that revealed someone's prejudice *toward* our side: "Ms. Burch, would your arrest at that public protest three years ago, make it hard for you to sit in judgment on this case and base your verdict solely on the evidence and law?"

"Campbell!" whispered Cullen in my ear, "Are you nuts? That's one juror who will see the case our way!" I responded, "I know and that's exactly why Rick Shaw will later knock her from the box. But my question will convey to other jurors that we're trying to be fair."

Years later courthouse gods raised new sabers of efficiency. They cut out the practice— and the adversarial nature— of prolonged juror questioning. Nowadays in many courtrooms judges ask the questions on voir dire.

But not then. Sometimes Shaw jumped to his feet, objecting to my barbed or loaded query: "Mr. Campbell's question doesn't go to whether this potential juror can be fair."

Each time my parry was the same: "Judge Cuttles, the answer to this question will determine how I exercise my clients' peremptory challenges."

Some background for this strategy. Trials arm attorneys with two ways to strike potential jurors from the box. One is "for cause," which means the person's answer clearly shows her prejudice.

The other is "peremptorily," for which no reason need be given. When "exercising a perem," attorneys simply ride their hunch the person won't look kindly on their client's case.

In our trial each defendant was allotted five peremptories. Nineteen clients meant perems combined to ninety-five, enough to sculpt a jury leaning toward our side.

Rick Shaw also clutched perems, but since he only had one "client," normally he'd only get a handful. Cuttles coaxed us to agree his number should be raised. But the prosecutor's total still was less than those who faced the prospect of a grey-bar home.

Back then lawyers with rich clients utilized two other jury-picking tactics: One was to employ detectives to investigate each juror candidate— to probe into the person's background, psyche, outlook, and other hints about the juror's mind.

Another method was to hire a consultant who could "read" a juror in the courtroom from the person's body language, dress, behavior, and responses on voir dire.

Both forms of extravagance lay far outside my clients'
pocketbooks. So I tried a Scottish way to ferret out some
clues: "Ms. Blankenship, do your family vehicles display
decals, bumper stickers— or words on frames around their
license plates?"

My goal was to find what kinds of humor, sports teams,
politics, or religious views their family felt the need to air
for fellow travelers on our roads.

I asked that question of our first twenty-seven candidates.
To my surprise, all but two denied their cars possessed a
single sign with words or symbols. From what I'd seen
each day on California cars, those denials seemed
statistically absurd.

But we had no resources to rebut these sworn assertions.
So next time a would-be juror brushed aside my query with
a stolid "No," I threw my shoulders back and joined the
courtroom laughter: "Guess I won't ask *that* again!"

As voir dire wore on, what intrigued me was Rick Shaw's
withholding his perems. Each time we closed a round of
questioning twelve candidates, I exercised a few perems.
But Shaw repeated the same litany: "The People find no
objection to this fine group of citizens."

Eventually my warrior thought he glimpsed Shaw's strategy.
At first he'd seem to stand on higher moral ground than
ours, implying any San Diegan would be fair.

But, warrior figured, Shaw would wait until our side had
whittled down the panel to twelve people who could see
our point of view; then he'd cast all of his perems to banish
them from court.

Near the middle of our second voir dire day we'd finished
one more round of questioning a dozen candidates. Our
side had settled on five folks we liked.

Once more Rick Shaw waived perems, chanting his ingratiating mantra of accepting any citizen. That meant our chosen five were safe from him until the final round.

But the next twelve candidates revealed what appeared to be a god-send to our side. A married, college-educated woman in her sixties stood up straight and gave expansive answers to all questions by both sides.

Forthright about her liberal politics, she volunteered: "During the 1950s, before Martin Luther King, Jr. began making headlines, I rode freedom buses into Deep South states. After that I signed up for the Peace Corps and worked abroad two years."

I shot a wide-eyed look at both co-counsel, telegraphing, *Oh man— we've got to have this person on our panel!* Instantly my warrior hit upon a plan to keep her on our jury and derail Rick Shaw's strategy.

When that round of questioning was done I asked Judge Cuttles for a brief recess to parley with my clients. All three lawyers for defense recognized the freedom-rider's presence as a stroke of luck. But it took me a quarter-hour to persuade our clients not to strike a single person in this group.

I reminded them how Shaw had waved his high-ground wand at every set of twelve. "His game must be to hoard perems until we've got a dozen jurors we desire. Then he'll use all his to decimate our choices. If we don't strike a single person in this set, we'll encourage his routine of agreeing to all twelve."

In a whisper I continued, "But this time his words will mean that he accepts the same folks we just did— and that will end voir dire! He'll not be able to cast a single one of his perems, especially against the one he fears the most: our freedom-riding, Peace Corps volunteer."

"What if he doesn't take the bait?" intoned one client under furrowed brows. "Why leave six others on the panel, ones we might not like or just aren't sure about? Shouldn't we at least strike them?" Other clients nodded at this less-risky strategy.

I said, "If you want that freedom-rider— and we surely do— this is our best chance to save her from perems by Shaw." Reluctantly my clients murmured, "Well, okay," and settled in their seats.

Judge Cuttles cleared his throat a fourth time, asking if defense accepted all twelve jurors in the box. For once we didn't reach into our bulging bag of challenges. Neither did Rick Shaw. Bingo— our jury of eight women and four men was set.

Final tally? Five jurors leaned toward the defense and six were pure unknowns— but our favorite one had walked or ridden many public-protest miles. Little did I know the way this juror's history would affect the outcome of our trial.

VII: PROSECUTION WITNESSES

"It's weird, isn't it, when you can't tell the good guys from the bad?"— Michael Connelly

In pretrial hearings the judge had blown away our five defenses: Nuremberg, Necessity, Crime Prevention, Innocent Intent, and First Amendment.

There remained a single issue for this trial: Was the missile factory's twenty-acre parking lot "open to the public?" If it was, my clients were not trespassers. Freedom lawyer quipped in mock heroics: *What a slender point on which to hang our planet's destiny!*

A story in the L.A. TIMES called our courtroom dance upon this legal thumbtack "colorful and sometimes humorous." For defendants, each day being watched and interviewed by members of the press provided opportunities to drill their anti-missile message into minds of fellow citizens.

Freedom lawyer saw it as a win-win situation for our side. Either the protestors would win freedom and publicity at trial or we'd change the law by our appeal of defenses scuttled by the judge.

Before Shaw started offering evidence, I moved to clarify the standard by which jurors would determine what was "open to the public." Shaw proposed to add one word: "open to the *general* public."

My clients would be favored by a definition framed in negatives. I urged "*not closed* to members of the public, so reasonable people would believe *no permission* was required to enter."

Judge Cuttles melded both our views. The jury would decide if the parking lot was "open to the general public— that is, would a reasonable person believe no permission was required to enter or remain."

Shaw placed the weight of his entire case upon the shoulders of one man: Lars Molesworth, chief of plant security. But this witness drove to court with truckloads of forensic evidence; he'd be FedEx for the prosecution's side.

When Shaw called his name, Molesworth strode across the courtroom toward the witness chair. He was a wiry man, early thirties, black hair parted on the left side of a largish head. When he spoke his voice was rough as burlap bags; he measured out his words like one accustomed to command.

His initial testimony came as no surprise: He claimed the missile-making premises— including the surrounding parking lot— was "private property and not open to the public." He had issued orders to his cadre of gendarmes to keep it so.

At the prosecutor's invitation, Molesworth stepped down from the witness chair and stood beside an easel Shaw had propped before the jury box. On it sat a cardboard schema of the parking lot and factory from an aerial view.

With Shaw's prompting, the witness slapped red Xs upon
seven spots he said bore signs proclaiming, "RIGHT TO
PASS BY PERMISSION, SUBJECT TO CONTROL." Next he
scratched on purple Xs indicating three official entries to
the parking lot.

Molesworth testified these three entrances bore one-by-two-
foot signs: "PRIVATE ROAD: NO ENTRY WITHOUT
PERMISSION." Beneath each was printed a citation to
California's Sabotage Prevention Act.

Defendants were not charged with sabotage, a crime that
could drop heavy penalties on unauthorized folks found
upon the factory's property. Although the act was scarcely
used by prosecutors, Shaw would later yank it out of
hibernation and shove it towards our witnesses.

Molesworth next identified nine photographs he'd taken
from the tarmac. They depicted entrance signs and
cameras placed strategically on building tops. He said his
surveillance gadgets didn't make recordings but were
always monitored by guards inside the plant.

Asking his star witness to resume the witness chair, Shaw
handed him a six-page memorandum. Yes, the man had
drafted it, dispatching copies to his underlings. Among its
guidelines and commands, the memo detailed how his
corps of cops must halt each stranger on the premises.

"My guards ask every visitor for I.D. and the reason for
their trip. If their purposes are not legit, we arrest them.
Only guests with clearances ranked 'secret' or at least
'confidential' can remain."

Rick Shaw quick-stepped to a film projector on the
prosecutor's desk. It was pointed at a tri-pod movie screen,
placed to capture images for jurors, clients, counsel, judge,
and people in the gallery.

I stood up. "Your honor, will the court ask Mr. Shaw what
he plans to unleash now?" The judge raised his eyebrows
at the prosecutor.

Shaw replied, "I'm cueing up a video of defendants' mass arrest. Since Mr. Molesworth took the video, I'd like him to provide a voice-over narrative of the event."

"I object, your honor. We've stipulated to my clients' peaceful arrest upon the parking lot."

"Sustained," sighed Cuttles, as if relieved to rule out Rick Shaw's over-kill. "In that event," the prosecutor said, sitting down, "I have nothing further from this witness."

Now came my turn to cross-examine Molesworth. From what the man had said— and failed to say— my warrior placed him on an information line somewhere between a pit bull and a bag of rocks. First I aimed to bring out facts that favored our defense.

Q. Mr. Molesworth, did we hear you right: there are no gates or fences anywhere around the parking lot, just a four-inch rounded lip of asphalt everywhere around its edge?

A. Yes, sir. That's correct.

Q. And is it true, despite your three marked entrances, most of the plant's 5000 workers come and go by driving over that lip at any point all around the lot's perimeter?

A. Yes, that's true. During shift-changes it saves a lot of time to let their cars and trucks just come and go that way.

Good man, warrior mused. *Got a firm grasp on the obvious.*

Q. And on that entire twenty acres of tarmac only seven signs assert the lot is private?

A. Yes, sir. We figured that was all we'd need.

Q. But not one said, "NO TRESPASSING"?

A. Well, yes, that's true.

Okay, warrior thought, *Molesworth, you still believe your kingdom's safe. Let's see what else you know— or don't.*

I set the scene so we could later prove one or the other of two useful points, maybe even both: Either there were gaping holes in plant security, or its chief possessed colossal ignorance.

Q. In the six-page memo of instruction to your guards is there any reference to allowing people to throw parties, fix their cars, or load their kids in buses on the factory's parking lot?

A. No sir.

Q. And that's because, as far as you're concerned, those events just don't occur?

A. That's right.

Q. Are all these measures guaranteeing plant security in force *after* working-hours at the plant?

A. Yes, sir. Seven days a week, twenty-four hours a day.

Q. So your guards would not allow outsiders to bring chairs or drinks or food onto the lot and have a party there?

A. No, sir, absolutely not.

Q. And they wouldn't ever let people from the neighborhood drive their cars and trucks upon the lot to make repairs and change their oil?

A. No way.

Q. Would they allow school buses on the lot to load and unload kids for girl-and boy-scout outings, along with parents and their cars?

A. No, sir, that would not be allowed.

Q. You testified your roof-top cameras are arranged so they can see the entire lot— is that correct?

A. Yes, sir.

Q. So guards who monitor these cameras twenty-four-seven would let you know if strangers tried to party, fix their cars, change their oil, or load up buses on the parking lot?

A. Yes, sir, they would.

Q. And your orders were to bust such people or at least kick them off?

A. Definitely.

Q. What about our city's public buses? Can they drive onto the parking lot to pick up members of the public or discharge them there?

A. No, Mr. Campbell, that's not permitted.

Q. What about the general public, Mr. Molesworth— are they allowed to drive their cars onto the lot and walk inside the plant's front lobby without being challenged for I.D. and special clearances?

A. No, sir. They'd be challenged as to who they are and why they came upon our premises.

Q. Thank you, Mr. Molesworth. I have no further questions.

VIII: DEFENSE WITNESSES

If you can't get up, get down.
If you can't get across, get across.
— Yiddish proverb

A weekend intervened before we put on witnesses. Earlier I'd asked the judge if I could drive my car upon the parking lot to better understand the set-up there. Over Shaw's objection, Cuttles said I could.

With co-counsel Bezelle Chatsworth as a front-seat witness, that Saturday I drove my old white Porsche to the missile plant. Deliberately avoiding an official entrance, I eased my wheels over the extended lip of blacktop that stretched around the twenty-acre lot.

Just as Molesworth testified, except for painted parking stripes, that four-inch elevation was the only indication that the tarmac wasn't part of the surrounding streets. We found no curbs, walls, or chain-link fences; no entrance gates, guard houses, or wooden arms that raised and lowered for each vehicle.

Of course! I thought. *They're trying to project the image of a peaceful little business, not a garrison assembling missiles that can decimate humanity. Plus, as Molesworth said, its curved edges let their workers come and go with more efficiency.*

Slow as a funeral train, Bezelle and I motored round the nearly empty lot. We spotted hooded eyes of rooftop cameras aimed directly at us, lenses slowly swiveling to keep our car in sight.

I paused my Porsche half a dozen times while Bezelle trained a pair of big binoculars at each building— our test to see if we'd provoke a "security response."

No buzzers or alarms; no warnings from loud speakers; not a single guard appeared. After fifteen minutes we drove off. I was eager to return to court and share this information with our jury.

But that weekend bad news also struck. Phones reached out and touched our steakhouse personnel. Cloaked in anonymity, callers warned our witnesses they'd lose their jobs if they divulged in court that they'd held after-hour parties on the parking lot. Fearing for their livelihoods, one by one these witnesses begged off.

Warrior slammed his fist into my palm: *Good God, our tightly woven strategy is fading like a discount rug! Should we subpoena all these folks and force them to the witness chair?*

Freedom lawyer added other questions: *Had plant personnel committed a new crime: obstructing justice by intimidating witnesses? Should I alert Judge Cuttles to this brazen felony? Should I pass this information to the press?*

But informing Cuttles or the media wouldn't wipe the fear out of our witness' minds. Moreover it would cause distraction and delay to hold extended hearings in the hope that we could find the source of those ad-terroram calls.

At least our waitress Eva Gladenstair hadn't bailed. Although divorced and raising two young kids on salary and tips, she still promised she would show.

I decided it was best to table all our options until Eva testified. If she came across as truthful and withstood Shaw's cross-exam, we could drop all counter-measures as unnecessary.

Monday I arrived at court and found my clients gathered in a circle just outside our courtroom door. Linking arms and swaying back and forth, they were serenely singing, "We Shall Overcome." Not one to scoff at solidarity, I joined in the group.

As soon as trial reconvened but before the bailiff led our jurors in, Judge Cuttles summoned me before his bench. A scowl replaced his normal placid countenance.

"Mr. Campbell, what is this I hear about a demonstration staged along the hallway of my court?"

"Your honor, with all due respect, it was not a demonstration— just a private indication of my clients' unity."

"I view it differently," the judge replied. "I take it as a

blatant effort to influence the jury. Furthermore I think you set it up."

"Judge, I freely joined my clients' circle of support but I knew nothing of it in advance. One thing I *did* know— when they softly sang their song in less than 60-seconds time— no jurors would be present. That's because you'd ordered them to report directly to the jury room down the hall, around the corner."

"Regardless, Mr. Campbell, if it happens one more time I'll hold you in contempt of court."

"Very well, your honor. I'll make sure I don't participate."

"No, Mr. Campbell, I don't mean just that. I mean no more courthouse demonstrations, period. If you can't control your clients I'll hold you in contempt for *that.*"

Warrior silently exclaimed, *Judge, what kangaroo got loose in your corral?! I doubt your powers of contempt can legally extend that far, but never mind. I'm sure defendants will comply.* So collapsed all courthouse gestures of my clients' camaraderie.

After jurors settled in their seats I called Eva Gladenstair as witness for defense. At thirty-five she strode across the courtroom in low heels, tan skirt, and a light brown sweater.

She sat straight as a bowstring in the witness chair; at first I worried she might freeze. But she relaxed when telling jurors how she'd been a waitress at the steakhouse for ten years. Blessed with what attorneys call an "affidavit face"— consummately trustworthy— she established crucial facts.

Eva testified about the nightly tailgate parties she and fellow workers held upon the factory's parking lot. She had also witnessed San Diego public buses drive onto the tarmac, stopping to take on and discharge passengers.

I paused to request Cuttles take judicial notice of three bus schedules I handed to him via his bailiff. Each showed city routes and stops upon the lot. Over Shaw's intense objection they were introduced as evidence.

Eva then resumed by saying nearly every time she worked a weekend shift she'd seen people park their private trucks and cars upon the lot to make repairs or change their oil. She'd also watched school buses there, surrounded by a dozen cars and sub-teen kids with overflowing duffel bags and backpacks.

"Thank you, Ms. Gladenstair," I said and took my seat. Freedom lawyer thought, *That evidence should clearly prove the parking lot was open to the general public. Let's see if Shaw can shake this veteran of obnoxious customers.*

Slow as sunrise, Rick Shaw rose for cross-exam. For twenty minutes he banged vainly at her testimony. A couple times he tried to bait her into an exaggeration of her views, so she wouldn't sound objective. Here too he failed to reach his mark. By the end he couldn't fluster Eva, couldn't trip her up, confuse her, even make her sound annoyed.

He did, however, raise one point that never got resolved.

Q. Isn't it a fact, Ms. Gladenstair, that over the ten-year span you said you and your friends had partied on the parking lot, now and then a guard from General Dynamics would come over to your group?

A. Yes, sir, but he never asked us to leave.

Q. Wasn't that because he saw your steakhouse uniforms and knew you had *authority* to park and party there?

I jumped to my feet: "Objection, your honor. Ms. Gladenstair can't see inside a plant guard's mind, nor can she know who did or didn't have authority."

"Objection sustained," Judge Cuttles ruled.

Puffed like a rooster with his back against the wind, Shaw aimed a final peck. "Is it not true, Ms. Gladenstair, that you support what these defendants were trying to do?"

"If you mean to save us from a nuclear war, you bet they've got my vote. But, Mr. Shaw, what I talked about today were simply things that took place on that parking lot. Why would I make up what so many other people saw as well?"

Right on, Eva! Warrior mutely whooped. *I couldn't* plan *a better ending to your testimony!* Shaw shook his head and headed toward his seat like Napoleon fleeing Moscow's freezing cold.

Eva did so well that we decided not to subpoena other steakhouse folks or try to prove who'd tampered with our witnesses.

Next I called Bezelle Chatsworth to the witness chair. Wearing a corduroy sports coat and blue dress-shirt with no tie, our former fire-fighter settled in the oaken seat.

Jurors chuckled when the lawyer said his role for the defense was "translating legalize to human-speak." My Porsche passenger two days ago, he related how we'd slowly reconnoitered round the factory's parking lot.

With some jurors leaning forward, Bezelle described loud-speakers mounted on each building. He'd spotted cameras trained on us from rooftops and related how their lenses followed every turn we made. Most jurors grinned when Bezelle said he'd tried to act suspicious, staring back at them through his binoculars.

Q. Did you hear anyone address us from those speakers?

A. No, sir, not a sound from them.

Q. Did anyone come out to stop us, ask us for identification, order us to leave, or place us under arrest?

A. No, not during the entire fifteen minutes that we drove around.

On cross exam the prosecutor tried to snag Bezelle in contradictions or embellishments but each time only caught the man's plain-spoken words. When Shaw ceased and took his seat, I thought about the fabled fox whose tricks had failed to snare a candid hare.

Allright, warrior whispered, *we've shown Molesworth testified from ignorance or fantasy. Now it's time to push our claim of "open to the public" one more step— from the parking lot into the plant itself.*

But when I called a student from my school to testify, Shaw jumped to his feet and pedaled swiftly to the judge's bench. "Your honor, I think Mr. Campbell better tell us what he wants to prove."

At sidebar I related that five law students and my school's receptionist had volunteered to drive to the factory during business hours, park upon the tarmac, and then walk toward the main building.

I continued, "Each one had a different experience but generally they'll testify they were not stopped, questioned for I.D., arrested, or kicked off. All were admitted to the guest-reception room. Most were handed pamphlets by employees; some sipped water from the office fountain; one even used a factory restroom."

As I laid out our case, Rick Shaw's face grew red with animation. When I finished, he insisted Cuttles read these witnesses their Fifth Amendment rights.

"What?!" I asked in disbelief. Surprise engulfed the judge as well.

"Because," Shaw said, "by coming on the premises of a secure facility without authorization each one violated our state's Sabotage Prevention Act."

Warrior muttered, *Brilliant tactic, Shaw!* But freedom lawyer ground his teeth. Of course, that act was cited on the factory's signs. But who would think— after years of letting uninvited members of public on these premises— Shaw would kick this sleeping California bear awake?

"Your honor, I commend the prosecutor for being so protective of the rights of people he might sometime wish to prosecute. But he's jeopardizing rights of litigants who need to prove their case today. This is clearly an attempt to scare our witnesses. For the sake of fairness and due process, your honor should insist the prosecutor state in good faith if he'll prosecute all witnesses who testify."

"Gentlemen," said Cuttles obviously concerned, "I'll dismiss our jury for the day and we'll discuss this matter in my chambers."

All jurors were released and all attorneys trailed Cuttles from the courtroom. The jurist stepped behind his maple desk stacked with squared-off heaps of papers. "Well, Mr. Shaw," said Cuttles, "are you serious about pressing charges on these witnesses?"

"Your honor, with all due respect, I must invoke the Separation of Powers doctrine. It shields prerogatives of the executive branch concerning when and if we'll prosecute."

Seeing storm clouds cluster on the judge's brow, Shaw quickly tacked his ship. "Your honor, I'm too low on the office totem pole to make such a serious decision. And right now my boss is out of town." With that he crossed his arms and shut up like a safe.

Shaw, my freedom-lawyer mused, *I'll buy your story when three piggies eat the moon! This statute's prosecutions are as rare as alligator fur.*

Cuttles' ire was unconcealed. "Mr. Shaw, I'll give you til tomorrow morning to find out if your office will invoke the sabotage— or any other— act against Mr. Campbell's witnesses. We'll meet in here at ten a.m."

* * * * *

Next morning Rick Shaw told us he'd discussed the matter with his boss and received authority to prosecute. However, Shaw himself had not decided if he'd exercise this power.

Rick, my warrior thought, *the last thing in the world I want to do is hurt you— but you're positively on my list.*

"Judge Cuttles," he said apologetically, "I'm afraid it's still a matter of prosecutorial discretion which, as you know, is relegated to the province of our government's executive branch."

"You needn't lecture me on constitutional law," snarled Cuttles. Thwarted in his order, the judge was clearly piqued. "Any suggestions, Mr. Campbell?"

"To make sure my clients get a fair trial— and avoid reversal on appeal— will the prosecutor grant my witnesses immunity?" The judge smiled, raised his brows, and looked expectantly at Shaw.

"Your honor, once again I'm sorry. Immunity is just the flipside of whether I should prosecute. At this time I'm simply not prepared to make that call."

Silently my warrior roared, *Shaw, you cluster headache, my dog wouldn't raise his hind leg on your shoe! Did you find some backdoor to escape from hell?*

"Very well, gentlemen," said an exasperated judge. "Unless one of you can find a route out of this impasse, I must instruct these witnesses of their right not to testify."

Before losing all my potent evidence, I grabbed a final straw: "Here's one suggestion, judge. Defense moves for a mistrial based on prosecutorial misconduct. Mr. Shaw has intimidated crucial defense witnesses and won't admit he's bluffing to secure a tactical advantage."

Shaw's face flashed instant crimson. But before he loosed a counter argument, Cuttles waved him off. "I'm afraid that remedy's too drastic. The prosecutor only wants me to advise your witnesses of their constitutional rights. It's not been shown that he's intimidated them."

"The result's exactly the same, your honor," I replied. "My witnesses fear dire consequences if they testify."

"Mr. Campbell, that's a choice they each must make. Your motion is denied." Walking back to court, I felt lonely as an asteroid and angry as a tethered cat.

* * * * *

Weeks later, mulling over this dilemma, I thought of what I might have done: Request a two-hour recess, draft new pleadings, and then speed to federal court.

Citing restoration statutes from the Civil War, I could have sought injunction of our trial, alleging federal due-process rights were being stymied by a prosecutor's threats.

Though doubtful any judge would issue an injunction, the publicity would have torn the cloak from Rick Shaw's ploy, exposing his strategic bluff. Shaw's boss might be forced to verify the obvious: City Attorneys don't indict inquiring missile-factory visitors for crimes of sabotage.

One month after trial I caught warrior juggling with this woulda-coulda-shoulda view. I shoved it in a time-vault, saying, *Every hard-fought Sunday rouses Monday morning quarterbacks; that's the way we learn.* But as I slammed the steel door, warrior mused, *There's not much hope in your career you'll ever get that chance again.*

* * * * *

Judge Cuttles reconvened proceedings. Before our jury entered, he directed my half-dozen witnesses to stand before his bench. Of course I'd told them of Shaw's tactic and their theoretical risk.

But Cuttles felt he had to place their warning on the record. So he announced, "I want to inform you of your Fifth Amendment privilege not to testify."

I interrupted. "Your honor, I'll stand with them. Since I asked them to visit the missile plant, I'm as much at risk as they."

Shaw's tactic worked. Of my students all but one withdrew to tight-lipped havens: "I'm sorry, Prof. I can't rest my law career on whether someday I'll be charged with sabotage."

"I completely understand," I told each one. "Thanks for your attempt to help."

Our non-witnesses trudged back to the gallery to join others from my school. Some students had appeared each day to show support and see what they could learn.

As soon as jurors took their seats behind the paneled barricade, I called the one brave scholar who would testify. In his second year of law, Josh Clarves walked with caution to the witness chair. He looked like a football cornerback watching upfield for the center's snap.

He told the jury he'd parked on the factory's lot for thirty minutes during business hours, sitting in his car to read the NEW YORK TIMES. Then he exited his car, walked slowly to a building labeled "VISITORS," and— unchallenged— stepped inside.

Clarves asked for any pamphlets that would tell about the factory's work. He was handed two brochures extolling guided missiles as a bulwark of our national defense. At no time did anyone ask him for I.D. or the purpose of his visit.

On cross-examination Shaw asked Clarves if he'd seen a warning sign upon the lot about the California Sabotage Prevention Act.

"Yes, I did," he said, leveling his steady gaze upon the prosecutor.

"No further questions for this witness," Shaw replied and took his seat.

Warrior scoffed: *Shaw, keep trying to intimidate my witnesses, you creep. It's obvious you can't score on cross-exam and you're scared that every factory-visitor who testifies will kick your losing case another ten-yards down the road.*

Our next witness was my school's receptionist. Uncowed by threats of prosecution, the tall, slim, thirty-one-year-old boldly stepped across the courtroom floor and sat down in the witness chair.

Sara Sojourn told the jury how she'd also driven on the factory's tarmac, left her car, and moseyed to the building marked for visitors. She went inside— again sans confrontation from security.

Sara asked a woman at the front desk, "Just what is it you guys do?" She was promptly given pamphlets to peruse. Another plant employee followed up by asking, "Do you have a question we can help you with?" Sara told her No and left.

On cross Rick Shaw aimed to show the jury Sara was a puppet for defense: "Isn't it true, Ms. Sojourn, that it was Mr. Campbell who directed you to go to the parking lot and try to get inside the plant?"

"No, that isn't true," Sara answered. "I *asked* Professor Campbell if there was anything I could do to help his clients' cause. He *suggested* I could drive to the missile plant and see if they would let me park and walk in as a member of the public."

As the afternoon drew on, Judge Cuttles said he had to deal with another matter. Noting members of the press were in the gallery, he admonished jurors not to read, hear, watch or talk about our case. Then he dismissed them for the day.

Next morning Shaw objected to some media accounts that claimed he'd tried intimidating witnesses. I hadn't mentioned this but journalists had seen my students warned in court and apparently arrived at this conclusion on their own.

Judge Cuttles didn't look at all disturbed. Perhaps he felt the same response my freedom lawyer did: *Shaw, you clearly brought that on yourself. I wouldn't wrap a dead rat inside your predicament.*

"But," the prosecutor said, "I'd like the court to warn Mr. Campbell not to mention any of this before the jury."

"I'm tempted but I won't," I said.

Our last witness was a defendant collectively elected as a witness for our group. Blanca Cumberpatch was a retired social worker and school teacher, plus she'd worked fifteen years as a probation officer. With the measured steps and poise of middle-age, she walked across the courtroom in a modest green-tweed suit.

Blanca testified that when she'd been a teacher, she'd bussed school kids to the missile factory to participate in guided tours. After her arrest for protesting she'd returned twice more.

The first time was a weekday about 6 p.m. Blanca parked her car— unchallenged— a few yards from the visitors' reception room. She saw a guard about to step inside the door and asked if he had any pamphlets he would share. He found one, gave it to her with a smile, and said, "This is all I have. Please, come back during business hours and get more from folks inside."

She returned next day with her husband. Inside the reception room both were handed plant brochures. But this time my client was accosted by none other than Lars

Molesworth, chief of plant security. The man demanded both of them produce I.Ds.

When they showed reluctance, Molesworth snapped, "You two are under arrest!" He ordered them to sit in chairs against the wall while he telephoned police. Blanca and her husband fished out drivers' licenses and held them in the air. Molesworth glanced at them and— to her surprise— said they both could leave.

On cross-exam Shaw probed every part of Blanca's last encounter at the plant. No doubt he wanted to impress the jury with the single instance when security had challenged someone on its premises. Point by point he dragged her twice across the confrontation scene but could shake loose nothing further that would help the prosecution's side.

When Shaw finished with Ms. Cumberpatch, she rose from the witness chair and joined her comrades on the front row of the gallery. I stood and said, "Your honor, the defendants rest."

IX: FINAL ARGUMENTS

Barristers' speeches vanish quicker than Chinese dinners, and even the greatest victory in court rarely survives longer than next Sunday's papers.— John Mortimer

In pretrial rulings Judge Cuttles had disallowed our defenses of Nuremberg, Necessity, Crime Prevention, First Amendment, and Intent. So both sides' arguments had to center on a single spot: Under California trespass law, had the missile factory's parking lot been open to the public? For three courtroom days our trial had been gnawing on this point.

On that issue rested victory or defeat. I figured post-trial news would conflate the outcome with my clients' larger aims as well as all their barred defenses. Then— with typical reductionism— the verdict would be touted as the city's recognition or rejection of defendants' cause plus legal reasons that had never reached the jury's ears.

On the eve of final arguments I stayed up late to organize my thoughts. I recalled how Shaw and I initially had spent hours exposing jurors to the Armageddon context of this trial. We'd sparred with voir dire hypotheticals— ostensibly to pick a jury— before we'd introduced a pebble's weight of evidence.

But with voir dire done and our defenses stricken as invalid, Judge Cuttles stood four-square: There'd no longer be a whisper about *why* defendants sat upon that parking lot.

Strategizing my summation, I heard warring voices in my mind. Freedom lawyer argued, *Don't you owe it to your clients and their cause to remind our jury of the larger voir-dire view? Wasn't that the reason the defendants risked arrest? Wasn't that precisely why they chose you as their lawyer— so you'd bring their message into court?*

A new voice intervened. Law professor pointed out, *You set your clients' issues into legal frames and battled fiercely for each one pretrial. Although rejecting them, Cuttles let you build a solid record out of facts and law. Now their proper place is on appeal. If you try to sneak them into final argument, the judge will cut you off. If you persist, he'll cite you for contempt of court.*

Warrior answered: *Art, you've risked contempt before, defending clients' rights. Throughout the long weeks of this case you've fought for freedom law against the force of mindless global politics that threaten to annihilate humanity. Why in hell stop now?*

These voices argued far into the night and later stomped through all my dreams.

Next day Dru and I drove downtown to the court. She took a seat beside her fellow demonstrators in the front row of the gallery while I parked myself at counsel's desk.

For a moment our eyes met. Warrior's charger nuzzled me: *Savor this chivalric view of People versus Drusilla Campbell: You're jousting for the honor of your wife against the state of California.*

Then another mock-heroic notion shook his reins: *Why not kick this up a notch? Imagine you're about to battle for the human race!*

Because the prosecution had to prove its case beyond a reasonable doubt, Rick Shaw got to argue twice: once before and once behind the lawyer for defense. From his chair five feet from me Shaw rose, straight as a flagpole, and tugged down his navy pin-striped vest.

It didn't take him long to highlight all the evidence he'd introduced through the plant's chief of security. He back-combed Molesworth's testimony, his memorandum, photographs, and marks on charts. "Surely, ladies and gentlemen, when you think about this mass of evidence, you can't conclude that parking lot was open to the public."

Then he loosed an arrow at the wall of our defense: "Remember Eva Gladenstair, that waitress from the steakhouse? When I questioned her, she admitted guards from the plant sometimes came around as they were partying. Isn't it a reasonable conclusion that guards let them carry on because those folks were *authorized* to use that section of the parking lot?"

Shaw paced to one end of the jury box, turned, and fired another shot. "What about that law student Mr. Campbell had drive to the plant? Like other witnesses Mr. Campbell sent, that person wasn't *invited* to enter. What if you throw a party for invited friends and a party-crasher comes inside your house— does that transform your home from private property to a place that's open to the public? That's what Mr. Campbell claims."

As if this observation clearly led to triumph for his side, Shaw smiled, gave a slight bow to the jury, and resumed his seat.

I rose for what would likely be the final jury argument of my career. I'd memorized the names and faces of our jury, so I began by looking at the countenance of juror number one. "Good morning, Mr. Jarvis," I said genially. "Good morning, Mr. Campbell," he replied.

I greeted every juror, using his or her last name. Each responded with respect. Then I placed myself before the middle of the jury box, took a slow breath, and began.

"The issue *isn't* about nuclear war and the devastation it can cause. And it *isn't* that my clients felt so committed to preventing world annihilation that they put their bodies on the line."

Warrior: *So far no objection or judicial warning. Time to step away and score some trespass points.*

"Please, don't be confused by what my learned opposition told you about *private* property— yours, mine, or the missile plant's. From this trial's very start my clients have agreed that parking lot was *private*. That's not an issue in this case.

"The legal issue's simply this: Was that unfenced asphalt *open to the public?* As Judge Cuttles will instruct you, that means would a reasonable person believe she would be free to enter there or stay?

"And here's the key to unlock all this trial's evidence, the lens that makes all viewpoints clear: It's not what the missile plant and Mr. Molesworth *thought* was true, but what they *did*. From everything you've heard or seen through this entire case it's only what they *did* that counts."

Freedom lawyer took an instant stock of things: *There, regardless of what happens next, the jury's heard my basic argument. It should frame Shaw's case inside a fantasy and snap ours into real life. Now let's praise the prosecution's only witness as an honest man.*

"Lars Molesworth tried to do his best to deal with a tricky task. He had to justify his job as well as prove the prosecution's case. So naturally he viewed all facets of security as he *thought* they were— not what really *happened* at the factory."

"Remember how he testified for Mr. Shaw that his plant had three official entrances? But what did he admit to me on cross-exam? Plant workers *really* used scores and scores of entry points— all around the lot's 8,000-foot perimeter.

"Mr. Molesworth also *thought* he had strict policies: His guards must challenge anyone who wasn't authorized to set foot on the premises. But when I questioned him on cross-exam, he failed to know what really *did* occur: years of party-goers from the restaurant across the street.

"Despite his staunch *belief* no city buses picked up public passengers and discharged them on the tarmac, three San Diego bus lines really *did*. Despite his claim of hourly patrols each day, seven days a week, he didn't know of weekend oil-changers, scouts, or parents' cars.

"Last weekend no one stopped my own suspicious foreign car, driving slowly, someone checking out his buildings with binoculars.

"In spite of signs and policies that Mr. Molesworth *thought* would keep out public visitors, there'd been tours by high-school students. Despite guards he *thought* would ask all strangers for their purpose and I.D., my school's receptionist and a student parked and walked unchallenged right inside one building."

Warrior tugged for my attention: *Time to grab a little flag Shaw waved and march it down a risky road.*

"The prosecutor told you of the day of protest, arguing that all those folks who *didn't* go onto the parking lot stayed away because they knew it wasn't open to the public. But I say these passers-by were merely folks my clients were *addressing*, ones defendants tried to *warn* by saying, 'Here's the place that makes the weapons that will end up killing you'."

"Objection!" Rick Shaw yelled. "Sustained," replied the judge.

Warrior: *Okay, I'll stop for now but how much further can I go before I step off Cuttle's cliff-edge of contempt?*

"Look again at what the factory really *did* instead of what chief Molesworth *thought* it did. I submit the factory's actions showed its parking lot was not *just* open to the public— but the factory even *wanted* it to be.

"Why else did the plant routinely let the general public on its parking lot and even in its lobby? So it would look like just another business and could hand out propaganda to persuade the public this was so. That's why it conducted tours for children of our *public* schools. That's why they let my *public* witnesses inside.

"Why did the factory leave its tarmac open to so many *other* members of the public? So it would look like a good neighbor to those folks you heard about: party-goers from the steakhouse, San Diego city buses, cabbies, people changing oil, working on their cars— Girl Scouts, Boy Scouts, and their moms and dads."

"But occasionally they *wished* they were not open to the public. They *wished* they were not open to the folks that dared to *challenge* what they made inside, those who *knew* what nuclear missiles do, those who knew the *danger*."

Shaw threw his pen down on his pad and started rising to object. I swiveled, faced him, and proceeded: "The missile factory wants it both ways. With one hand they greet the public to promote a benign image and keep filling up their coffers with our taxes. That's why they don't use fences, gates, or seriously police their grounds.

"With the other hand they want to block out folks who dare to say, 'What you're doing threatens life upon this planet'."

I saw Shaw start to rise again. Glancing at the judge, I read warning from his lowered brows: *You're tugging at my patience, counselor. My gavel's just eight inches from my hand and it will thump you with contempt.*

But I took another step in the direction I'd been heading: "Let's look at *real* life. The missile factory *thinks* that it's so powerful it doesn't need gates, fences, or consistent policies about security. It just arrests the folks it doesn't like. So many people stay away... or think nuclear missiles are not dangerous... or just don't think at all."

"Mr. Campbell," cautioned Cuttles, "stick to the facts in evidence."

Warrior: *Okay, he's warned me on the record. He's laid footers for his hammer of contempt. But his tone seemed milder than expected; perhaps he's leaving room to escalate. That means I've got a few more steps before I reach his cliff. I'll save them until later; right now let's change the route.*

I reminded jurors of our courtroom rules: that this would be my only time to speak to them. In the prosecutor's final turn he might raise some points I wouldn't be allowed to counter. "But *you* can counter them. The evidence you've seen and heard has all the answers you will need."

I listed arguments that "Mr. Shaw *might* make. He might toss around scare tactics like he used against you on voir dire— that you'll need to build a fence around your home if you declare the missile factory's parking lot was open to the public."

I looked at Shaw, staring at me fiercely, chin propped on his fists. He changed to a non-committal gaze.

"But no *reasonable* person would conclude that by leaving your home unfenced or front door unlocked, you've
164

somehow made it open to the public. And, as Judge Cuttles will tell you, that's the legal test— what a *reasonable* person would believe.

"On the other hand, if you let strangers change their oil in your driveway, walk casually inside your house, sit down on your couch, and you give them pamphlets— all without confronting them— then you *should* be worried. That's exactly why the missile plant is scared."

Warrior nudged me: *Time to slip another client message in.*

"And if you make guided missiles in your home— threatening our planet— you *should* worry that some neighbors might protest, might want to tell the world what's going on."

"Objection!" shouted Shaw, bristling like a patch of cactus. Judge Cuttles scowled but in a measured tone repeated, "Mr. Campbell, confine your arguments to the evidence."

I stepped back to my prior path. "The prosecution has implied my law-school witnesses— the ones who walked into the lobby of the plant— were sneaks or spies. But I submit those witnesses were *demonstrators.* They demonstrated to *you* the difference between what the factory really *did*— in stark contrast to what Mr. Molesworth *thought* it did.

"The able prosecutor may argue that my clients should act like adults and take their medicine; he might say they broke the law and should be willing to be punished. But, let me remind you, they did not protest the *trespass* law. They protested the appalling specter of nuclear war...."

"Objection!" roared Rick Shaw. Judge Cuttles glared at me before turning to the jury. "Ladies and gentlemen, defendants' reasons for protesting are not before the jury. Mr. Campbell, this court admonishes you to stick to the evidence."

I took a deep breath and continued: "Our nation doesn't just *permit* protesting. Our country *requires* it. Let me take you back to one hot Philadelphia summer in 1787. Benjamin Franklin is emerging from a building where the Founding Fathers signed our nation's brand-new Constitution."

I glanced at Shaw, his butt poised on the front edge of his chair. "A worried woman walks up to Mr. Franklin and asks, 'Sir, what kind of country have you given us?' Franklin answers, 'A democracy, madam— if you can keep it.'

"That's what my clients were trying to do, preserve our democratic way of life, arouse a citizenry that was unaware…"

Cuttles: "Mr. Campbell, this is the last time I'm going to warn you!"

Warrior: *Okay, I've reached his cliff-edge. In a moment I'll risk one more step. But first I must remind the jury what we want.*

I walked slowly from the middle of the courtroom to a spot ten feet from the center of the jury box. "Let's be clear about one thing: My clients aren't *protesting* trespass law today— just the opposite. They're *invoking* trespass law. We're asking you to *follow* trespass law.

"We want you to declare exactly what this trial's evidence has proved abundantly: *Reasonable* people would believe that parking lot was *open* to the public. Therefore my clients were *not* trespassers.

"Now let me leave you with a final thought, the words a famous soldier once delivered to his troops. The man was General George Washington. Standing before the Continental Army in 1783, here's what he said: 'If men are to be precluded from offering their sentiments on matters which may involve the most serious and alarming consequences to mankind…'"

166

"Same objection!" shouted Shaw.

"Overruled."

"… 'then reason is no use to us. Then freedom of speech may be taken away…'"

Shaw leapt to his feet: "Objection!"

"Let him finish," ruled the judge.

"… 'and dumb and silent we may be led like sheep to slaughter'."

"Objection! Objection!" bellowed Shaw.

But I was done. Lowering my voice, I said, "Thank you, ladies and gentlemen, for your patience and attention."

Sitting down, I wondered why Judge Cuttles let me finish the quotation. Warrior answered, *Can't you see? Now he's got a total record of contempt— all his warnings, your repeated disregard. Of course he'll steer clear of juror sympathy by not trouncing you right now. He'll wait until the jury's been sent out to deliberate— or maybe until after they come back.*

Rick Shaw stood to pitch his final argument, glowering with red-faced indignation. "Ladies and gentlemen, why do you think Mr. Campbell at every opportunity slipped one in on you about the end of the world, the fear of nuclear holocaust?"

Right on! warrior noiselessly applauded. *Keep reminding them!"*

Shaw continued, "Why? Because he's trying to cloud your minds, so you won't look at facts and listen to Judge Cuttles' instructions on the law.

"Propaganda!? He says the plant is spewing propaganda but that's just what *he's* done in court. He wants you to be scared, afraid of nuclear holocaust, the end of the world. If what he says is true, you might as well take off your juror badges. I should burn my suit and the judge should throw away his robe. All of us should simply hunker down in caves and await the end of the world."

Freedom lawyer thought, *Nice image, Shaw! I couldn't say it better— much less get away with it.*

Shaw stepped nearer to the jury box and released a risky argument. "Ladies and gentlemen, go ahead, acquit defendants if you believe that sympathy should rule the day. But then go home, build a fence around your property, and don't call the police if trespassers come— because you will have changed California law."

Now the prosecutor stalked before our jurors like a rampant bear. "But instead, let's look rationally at things. If you choose people of a certain religious or political persuasion to come onto your private property, that's your *choice*, your freedom of choice. You should retain that choice, not abandon it. Removing choice because of fear is the most classic form of propaganda. Please, don't fall for it."

Rick Shaw turned to glance at me then swung back to the jury box. In a solemn tone he finished strong: "Ladies and gentlemen, these defendants had their chance to bask in media attention, to bring their message to the public. They've enjoyed their fifteen minutes of fame. Now it's time for them to accept responsibility."

X. VERDICT

It's tough to make predictions,
especially about the future.
— Yogi Berra

When the prosecutor took his seat, freedom lawyer felt tape break across his chest as if he'd crossed a finish line: *Shaw didn't draw within ten yards of us— we've won!*

Warrior danced a jig of grandiosity: *I don't care if we get hammered for contempt— we spoke truth about the larger issues here. But even on the smaller point of trespass, we demolished Rick Shaw's case. How could any juror think that parking lot was not open to the public?*

Freedom lawyer added, *What a chance to make a difference in the worldwide fight to rein in nuclear arms— first courtroom victory of mass demonstrators! And handed down by San Diego jurors in a city nurtured by Marine and Navy bases— the very heart of "Missile Land." What encouragement to other activists! What a green light to protestors of the world!*

But I had to haul my forecasts from the clouds and focus on the job at hand. Cuttles, Shaw, and I now needed to resolve all points of law the judge would tell the jury.

This task, however, sparked no serious debate and consumed less than an hour's time. After jurors were instructed they trooped to their private room to decide my clients'— and who else's?— fate.

Once more freedom lawyer filled his sails with predictions: *We'll share our trial strategies with movement counsel coast to coast— send them copies of our pleadings about Nuremberg, Necessity, and Crime Prevention. Someday a court will recognize these defenses as legitimate.*

But, warrior pointed out, *our San Diego victory will have an even bigger impact from the fact we didn't use all those defenses—only brought the larger picture to a jury of our peers!*

Jurors huddled for about three hours. That matched the litigator's rule of thumb: one hour for each day of trial. But when I watched them trudge back to the jury box, instant dread extinguished all my confidence.

Each juror walked deliberately, staring at the floor. When they took their seats not one looked upon my clients; three female jurors wept. *Oh, god— all the classic signs of verdict for the prosecution!*

Judge Cuttles: "Ladies and gentlemen, have you selected a foreperson?" The freedom-rider stood and answered, "Yes, we have. It's me."

"And have you reached a unanimous verdict?"

"Yes, your honor. Guilty as charged."

As gasps exploded in the courtroom, my world fell apart.

* * * * *

From the outset I'd informed my clients of the worldwide implications of a courtroom win. But most of them— less grandiosely than their lawyer— remained focused on the group's initial goal: "Let's just get our message out to San Diego citizens."

Therefore many clients shrugged off proclamation of their guilt. Seemingly indifferent to the trial's impact on the planet's politics, their post-verdict task was plain: "How best reframe our Armageddon points for local media?"

My own statement to the press tried to drown my ego's devastation in a pool of saving face: "It's a little difficult to defend a case in missile-land when the judge prohibits five defenses and a sixth is blocked by threats from the prosecutor."

* * * * *

A few weeks later a client met one juror after services at church. "Do you feel okay sharing how you all decided we were guilty?"

The juror's face turned sorrowful. "Mr. Campbell had us all convinced the parking lot was open to the public, that you all were brave and shouldn't go to jail."

The juror took a breath and then went on: "But our foreperson told us all about her protests in the fifties, how her freedom-riders aimed to get convicted in the South. She felt what your movement needed were some martyrs for the cause. She said, despite your evidence and arguments, what you *really* needed was a guilty verdict."

XI. SENTENCES

Crime doesn't pay— or at any rate,
not for a very long time.
— John Mortimer

One month after trial the defendants, all still free on bail, reassembled in the courtroom. Many brought their friends and families; other people came to show allegiance to my clients' cause. Members of the press jostled elbows in the front seats of the gallery.

The question of the day: Would defendants get the statutory max of six-months jail and $500 fine? Both were in the realm of possibility, given the accuseds' deliberate defiance of the law, insistence on prolonged pretrial hearings, their singing in the hall, and contentious days of trial.

* * * * *

Last month, before conferring with defendants, my intention was to recommend probation for them all. But when I raised this with the group, it sparked another lengthy colloquy. They had to reach consensus on suggested outcomes for their long campaign.

Some clients thought integrity forbade requests for leniency. Others felt they couldn't honor what I said Judge Cuttles likely would require as condition for probation: that they not protest by trespass for a year.

At last we reached accord: I'd urge the group be sentenced to some form of public service. After making beaucoup phone calls, I compiled a list of thirteen charities who'd welcome help from people with my clients' capabilities.

They could tutor kids for every grade of school; screen candidates for various forms of help; gather and distribute food; sort, staple, stamp, and mail envelopes; etcetera.

Pro-bono service formed the tent-pole of my sentence memo to the court— pitched as an apt conclusion to this type of crime and my clients' public-service motives. I included brief biographies and individualized accounts of why each chose to protest at the missile plant.

What a difference from presentence memoranda I'd submitted in the past! Every client was or once had been a civic leader. Their bios sparkled with blue-ribbon resumes, awards, achievements, plus letters of support and praise from other people of distinction.

* * * * *

Judge Cuttles entered court, striding to his swivel chair behind the bench. His face displayed more than its usual solemnity. Warrior muttered, '*Zounds, I hope that look is for the press!*

The clerk called roll and each defendant answered, "Here, sir," "Present," or just "Yes."

Rick Shaw sat erect and smiling at the prosecutor's table, now swept clear of documents and files. He caught my glance and thrust his hand into his briefcase on the floor. He drew out a hardback book and stood it upright on his desk: LAW OF SENTENCING.

I felt a solar-plexus thud: it was the treatise I'd left Washington, D.C., to write. Freedom lawyer cursed: *Damn— I published arguments for defense and prosecution!*

"Mr. Campbell," said the judge, "I've read your sentence memorandum, your clients' biographies, and the reasons for their acts. I've also seen reports from the probation office, including each defendant's financial status."

Cuttles looked along the row of the accused: "I'll admit this court's impressed with the defendants' backgrounds, their leadership in our community, and sincere beliefs about the threat of nuclear war."

Turning back to me, he said, "I've also weighed your arguments for public service. Warrior whispered, *Uh-oh, that tone of voice shows he's not buying them.*

The judge continued, "However, Mr. Campbell, I'm inclined to place your clients— except two repeat offenders— on probation for one year, and impose a fine on each of an amount between $100 and $150."

Cuttles paused to let that statement penetrate the courtroom. "Probation would be based on two conditions: First, that each accused complete eight days of public service acceptable to the court; anyone who can't afford the fine must work three extra days.

"Second, each defendant will not violate the trespass statute— or any similar law— for one entire year. They'll still be free to exercise their First Amendment rights, just not break the law while doing so."

Freedom lawyer groaned, *Great Scot— he's echoing my former view about a sentence, one my clients didn't want! Since he can't impose probation without their consent, looks like we'll need another colloquy.*

Cuttles turned to me. "Mr. Campbell, would you like some time to confer with your clients?"

"Yes, your honor," I replied. We gathered round and shared impassioned whispers for ten minutes but could not reach consensus. I rose to my feet.

"May it please the court, my clients have a multitude of views. Would you hear briefly from each one and let them say again why each protested and who is willing to accept your terms?"

"That's agreeable," said Cuttles, "but first the court will deal with two defendants who have previous convictions for protesting while trespassing. Their earlier probation terms clearly didn't stop them from committing trespass once again."

In an eerie monotone Judge Cuttles sentenced two male clients to ninety days in county jail. A silent chill blew through the courtroom as deputies ratcheted handcuffs on these two and towed them out the door.

The judge looked down at Shaw. "Does the government wish to address the court about appropriate sentences for the other defendants?"

Rick Shaw stood. "Yes, your honor. But rather than suggest a disposition for each of the accused, the people will speak once."

He picked up my black-bound treatise. "Mr. Campbell literally wrote the book on sentencing and in it I discovered the most rational way to frame society's issues for this court."

Shaw flung a grin at me and then resumed: "Sentencing has four aims: deterrence, retribution, incapacitation, and rehabilitation. I doubt the last two goals can be attained within the statutory maximum of six months in jail."

Warrior muttered, *Nice flourish, Shaw— now what the blazes is your point?*

He continued: "But according to a case in Mr. Campbell's latest supplement, where defendants' acts are premeditated— as these were— a harsh sentence can be an effective *deterrent*."

Shaw leafed to another section of the book. "Finally, the professor says that retribution is another aim of sentencing. That rationale asserts that when defendants try to publicize their views by grabbing our society by the throat, it's right that they be punished. That's all I have to say."

For the next two hours Cuttles and the courtroom audience listened to impromptu testimonials from my clients about why they'd risked arrest to halt the race of nuclear arms.

One woman spoke through streaming tears. Cuttles asked if she would like to take a moment to compose herself. "That's all right, your honor. I always cry when I'm this serious."

Another client was a college senior. He marched to the podium and said, "Your honor, our defense of international law was rejected, thus rendering the Nuremberg trials meaningless. Indeed, this trial's issue came down to human rights versus property rights of a missile factory. That's the same false dichotomy that fuels the nuclear arms race."

Judge Cuttles scribbled on a yellow pad but his face remained expressionless.

When her turn came my wife Drusilla walked gravely to the courtroom microphone. She gripped both edges of the podium and described a haunting vision she could not wipe from her mind: "Our sons, five- and eight-years-old, are caught inside a sudden sky-searing flash. Knowing what it means, they run to us and ask, 'Mommy, Daddy, why didn't you and other grown-ups stop it'?"

In the end, despite their prior solidarity, all but four defendants chose probation on the judge's terms. However, two grandparents, a Catholic nun, and the outspoken college senior refused. They felt the court's conditions would be a moral compromise to their commitment to prevent the planet's rush toward self-annihilation.

Their rejection of probation triggered two surprising incidents. First, the prosecutor only urged ten days in jail for these folks. Second, Cuttles brushed aside Rick Shaw's implicit plea for clemency. Instead he sentenced my most conscientious clients to $150 fines and twenty-days in jail.

* * * * *

From our group's strategic view, harsh jail terms brought
new mission benefits; they sparked more coverage in the
news. Now some demonstrators had become true "martyrs
for the cause"— jailed for their efforts to avert earth's
final war.

Overall— from protest through to sentencing— my clients
reached their goal: media attention for their cause. One
journalist observed, "Today's protestor is mature, better
informed, and more determined than ever to save mankind
from nuclear nightmare."

My failed aims did not conflict with those of the accused.
I'd simply reached for much, much more. Thus knowing
that my clients actualized their goals did little to assuage
my private agony.

When asked by the press to share post-sentence sentiments,
my wounded warrior seized the microphone: "This has
been a dispiriting end to a very long road. Every criminal
defense lawyer is something of an optimist and an idealist.
I felt, if we could get a verdict in San Diego, our case would
have global impact."

Then freedom lawyer shoved his counterpart aside: "This is
the first grass-roots movement in years to be started by the
middle class. The end to the nuclear arms race is the
challenge of our times. The movement to stop the madness
is just beginning."

* * * * *

Next week I phoned Rick Shaw to give him notice I was
heading to Judge Cuttles' chambers. The prosecutor had a
right to counter my request to cut some clients' sentences.

"Which ones?" Shaw inquired. "The long-ball terms on both
grandparents and the nun. As a point of honor, the college
senior still won't ask for mercy."

"Good luck," Rick Shaw said with what seemed genuine sincerity. He elected not to show or register his opposition.

Inside the judge's chambers framed diplomas, photos, and awards looked down on just two souls: a jurist and a lawyer. Gone were courtroom crowds, stenographers, and journalists bent forward with their pens.

"Your honor, will you reduce three of my clients' sentences to the time they've spent in jail, plus twenty days of public service? Surely they've now paid for their five-minute trespass with a week's incarceration."

"Motion granted," Cuttles said without emotion and returned to reading papers on his desk.

As warrior exited he mused sardonically, *Ain't it grand how Justice sometimes readjusts her scales when relieved of weighty thoughts about the press and one's career?*

XII. APPEALS

Law and justice aren't the same.
— RAISING THE BAR

The first stop on our climb to higher courts was the Appellate Division of Superior Court. I thought Cuttles clearly erred by blocking our defenses of necessity and crime-prevention. I felt so strongly that I took the maverick tack of dropping every other claim to focus on these two.

My brief swelled to 50 pages since I needed to append the documents we'd introduced at trial: international treaties, scientific evidence, and judicially accepted facts about the carnage caused by nuclear bombs.

Imagine my surprise at later reading the appellate calendar, seeing I'd been granted just five minutes for an oral argument. Freedom-lawyer shook his head before this incongruity: *Terrific— five entire minutes to defend my clients and mankind!*

I recalled my virgin appellate argument, startling judges in a state supreme court when I stood before them as a student in my final law-school year. Warrior warned me: *This time don't start sparring with a judge!*

But when the clerk called "People versus Drusilla Campbell," I risked another breach of protocol: "May it please the court, since our brief contains such compound issues of constitutional and international law, may I ask if there is any point this court would like me to address?"

I watched for clues I'd ticked off any of the three appellate judges, rashly asking *them* a question instead of humbly waiting for vice-versa. The middle judge leaned toward his right, conferred, and then bent briefly to his left. All three nodded to each other and the center jurist turned to me.

"Mr. Campbell, I'll inform you now, this court has no issues to discuss. Your points were raised in a protest case we dealt with earlier. To be consistent, we've applied our holdings in that case to yours. In fact we've already printed copies of our opinion in your case, so you can hand one to each client. They're resting right here on our clerk's desk."

I felt pole-axed. Five minutes for my argument had seemed a cosmic irony but these words changed the task to farce. My sense of justice reeled from this mockery of law and my clients' righteous cause.

Under piercing eyes of fellow lawyers, I tried to stride with dignity across the courtroom to the designated desk. Hefting a small stack of stapled sheets, I marched to the exit door, staring straight ahead.

Outside I slumped on a hallway bench and scanned a copy of their ruling. Another shock: Summarizing every argument I'd raised, they merely marked each one "Denied" in an opinion three pages long!

178

Freedom lawyer hearkened back to law school days. My first trial had been held above a dry-goods store before a justice of the peace. *That was your introduction to the marriage of our law with politics. When do you expect this basic human trait to change?*

Through the mental maelstrom one more question buzz-sawed through my brain: *Where did those judges see these points before?*

Suddenly it struck me. Weeks ago I'd shared our pretrial motions with non-client members of the protest group. One man, who'd been arrested at a different time and place, later lost his trial without counsel after half a day in court.

Not consulting any lawyers of our team, he'd apparently appealed his conviction by rewording our defenses in lay terms. Like many folks who trusted in the law but not in lawyers, he believed his arguments would win by simply paraphrasing them.

Warrior cursed the nincompoop who coined the phrase, *res ipsa loquitur:* "the facts speak for themselves." *Good God, what judge could be persuaded by— or even grasp— these complex, novel points when thrown at them sans logic, caselaw, statutes, treaties, or essential facts accepted only by <u>our</u> trial court?!*

I'd spent weeks constructing factual foundations and precedents for our defenses of necessity and crime-prevention. These issues merited serious appellate scrutiny.

But by sharing written pleadings with a pro-se litigant, it was I who'd later let appellate judges pick an easy path through all our thorny points of law. Seeing them a second time, the jurists blew them off as clones of kooky protest fantasies.

Our next move was to petition California's intermediate appellate court. But it declined to hear our case— as did the state supremes.

We won a mini moral victory when Chief Justice Bird urged supreme-court colleagues to accept our case for argument. In dissent she asserted, "This is an important and critical issue for our state and our Republic. It should at least be given a chance to be debated."

Warrior urged, *Let's push this case a final step, the only one remaining in our quest for resolution of these points of law: Petition for review by the Supreme Court of the United States.*

I phoned freedom lawyers all across the land and asked for their advice. They laid it on me with surprising unanimity: "Please don't try it, Art. Not because the Court *won't* grant your case review but because it *might*."

They urged me to abide with their informal strategy: "Since political positions of the current bench would slaughter your defenses, that would kill them nationwide. At least now they're still alive in other states and can be argued case-by-case."

I drew warrior aside and told him we must face the truth: *It's time to drop our splintered lance. There're no more courtrooms left to change the outcome of this case.*

* * * * *

What do academics do when their ideas slam into brick walls of reality? They tuck them inside comfy covers of a law review. That's the route I took.

I confined my writing to our novel use of crime-prevention, re-titled to attract like-minded scholars and attorneys: "The Nuremberg Defense to Charges of Domestic Crime: A Non-Traditional Approach for Nuclear-Arms Protestors."

I didn't credit Richard Shaw for fathering that defense. Freedom lawyer winced a little at this oversight, but my wounded warrior hadn't healed.

For centuries courts have held that crime-prevention justifies what otherwise would be a common crime. This

logic should extend as well to those who try preventing
international crimes— especially those enshrined in treaties
that our nation signed.

XIII: WINNING

*The final key to one's survival is in handling
not the historical but one's personal past.*
— Larry McMurtry

*F*ollowing our vain appeals, nearly every night at two a.m.
warrior whacked me from my dreams: *You lost the trial
and let appellate judges duck its vital legal points! That
was your opportunity to make a real difference! You blew
the chance to use what you had learned from all your trials
and errors!*

When I rolled over, trying to ignore him, warrior slashed
me deeper with his whip of blame: *You spurred your
charger right past routes that would have led to victory! A
win at either trial or appeal would have slowed the race of
nuclear arms and made a lasting contribution to the law.*

Before I heard about the way a freedom-riding juror had
transformed our trial's triumph to defeat, I replayed our
trial scores of times: *Where did I go wrong? What should I
have done or left alone? What had I said or failed to say?*

Later learning of the juror only added to my midnight
clobbering. Like a poltergeist of blame, now warrior
walloped me because my risky jury-picking plan had
placed our trial's outcome in a single set of hands. The
freedom-rider's certainty our message needed martyrs had
convinced her peers to disregard the evidence and law.

Eventually my warrior's rage subsided and I returned to
what was real. I recognized his midnight saga of defeat—
like all his prior whoops of victory— was simply, merely,
only that: a *story.*

No single tale could embody my career or define my core. Indeed *any* story's lasting value doesn't spring from its portrayal of a plot or character but from pointing to what's real in its *reader's* heart.

* * * * *

More than a decade after we had jousted with such animosity, Rick Shaw faxed me at my school. "Art, that case we tried together years ago? Well, my friend, you won!"

I telephoned my former adversary: "Rick, what kind of bullshit are you slinging now?"

"No, I'm serious, Art. Let me prove it. Meet me today at noon outside the main gate to your school. I want to drive you somewhere in my car."

At twelve o'clock Shaw picked me up and took us to the parking lot where my clients had been busted. "See?" he asked and waved his upturned palm above the dashboard of his car. "Look around us, Art. The missile factory's gone. Your side finally won!"

He had a point: With less demand for nuclear arms, the missile plant had moved. Shaw paid for lunch inside the steakhouse where my friend and our defense's major witness used to work.

About that time my wife was called for jury duty. When asked if she had ever been arrested, Dru recapped her trespass at the missile plant. The judge smiled broadly and announced, "Well, ma'am, I guess you won."

Sometimes history changes slowly. At this writing there's been *some* reduction in our planet's stockpiled nukes. In that sense my clients' demonstrations and publicity— along with scores of other protests round the world— helped the human race at least slow down before it toppled off the precipice of self-destruction.

ENDGAME

We live the given life and not the planned.
— Wendell Berry

The protest trial made me reassess the arc of my career.
As litigation always had, preparation swallowed huge
amounts of time. Since the case's underpinnings stretched
to nearly half a year, they made my minutes in the
classroom welcomed respites from the constant regimen
of research, drafting, strategizing, and conducting client
conferences.

With all appeals finished and the law-review complete, I
found time again to taste the world beyond a litigator's fare.
While thumbing through a menu of philosophy, I stumbled
on another potent quote from William James:

"I am done with great things and big things, with great
institutions and big success. And I am for those tiny,
invisible, molecular moral forces that work from individual
to individual through the crannies of the world."

Voila! Framed and hung upon my office wall, these words
captured what I'd left behind and roused my appetite for
all that lay ahead. However, there were parts of me I
needed to align with this new point of view.

First I sat down for a parley over coffee with my freedom
lawyer. I told him not to think his labor of the last few
months had gone for naught: "Publishing that crime-
prevention article sent the issue out, waiting to be used by
someone, sometime, somewhere else."

"But," I said "you must accept the fact your scene's no
longer trials. You need to put to rest your fantasy that one
day we'll stride into court to cheers of 'Campbell's back!'"

Freedom lawyer stared beyond my shoulder, then looked
hard at me: *Okay, we both accept the fact each day's a little
death. But can you bury your enduring dream of solo
practice, San Francisco style?*

I replied, "It won't be easy but I will. It helps to feel the rush I get discussing law and life with students in my office and in class."

It also helped to recognize how lucky I had been. Few people get to actualize their childhood fantasies. Since six years old I'd dreamt someday I'd be a fighter seeking justice for the powerless.

On my deathbed I can smile, knowing I once felt the thrill of wielding words inside the coliseums we call courts. With one of my last breaths I'll cheer on lawyers marching round the world behind those banners I once gripped with so much passion.

Next I sat down with my warrior and a pitcher full of beer. After we each quaffed a mug, I looked him in the eye: "You've given me my life's peak moments. I've never felt so much alive as when speaking up for fellow travelers, championing their causes, rights, and dignity. But for me there's more to life than ceaseless preparation for mañana's courtroom combat."

Warrior sagged a moment, then looked up: *You can't make me disappear with just a finger snap— I'm entwined inside your DNA! You'll live with me until you die.... Hey, we'll still run races every weekend, right?*

His words were partly true: Deep inside I'd always live with warrior just as I'd forever be a freedom lawyer. "But there's something else we've got to face. After thirty years of pounding canyon floors and concrete streets, my creaky knees are giving out. Look again at the horizon; the day's approaching when road-races have to stop."

Warrior rumpled up his brow, slowly filled our mugs, and muttered, *Then what will we do?*

I said, "Remember when we both were kids and fancied we were rescuing somebody as we galloped through the forest on my father's horse? Let's continue racing— only let a *horse* provide our legs."

184

Warrior drained his glass: *I don't get it. We're too old for urging Thoroughbreds around a track. Are you thinking of endurance competitions, ones sometimes extending to a hundred miles? Now there's a real challenge— let's give it a try!*

So we bought an Arab stallion, called Zarahas, with bloodlines for long-distance runs. As we galloped into shape we often passed a polo field, each time pausing to observe man's fastest contact sport.

One day a player put his mallet in my hand. That was the final time we trained for an endurance race. Although Zarahas had to cowboy up to polo's sudden sprints, stops, pivots, bumps, and ride-offs, during every tournament my fighter dined on ecstasy.

* * * * *

Now that I'd rebalanced warrior and my freedom lawyer, I picked up the gauntlet thrown by Carl Jung: "The function in the second half of life is to sustain the culture that supported you in youth."

Time to pass on to my sons and students what I'd learned. With fresh vigor I returned to family and school. Although I didn't always brandish it with skill, I tried to ply the sword of truth, the only blade that heals as it cuts.

As once-divergent facets of my life merged into harmony, each year in the classroom saw me teach with more conviction and vitality.

Students sometimes rolled their eyes when I extolled careers of tossing pennyweights upon the Blind Dame's scales. I never promised pupils they would dance along a rainbow every day, but I knew they'd find fulfillment bringing freedom law to any legal field.

When I'd nearly finished writing up this trilogy, I read a classic tome on painting by a man called E.H. Gombrich. Like myself in this third book, the man had spent his life in search of ways to disengage "Art" from "Illusion."

185

His bottom line? "There is no way of finding out except by trial and error— by which I mean the double rhythm of lumbering advance and subsequent simplification."

That's been the underlying thesis of these books about my life at law— and is now my law of life. Every moment my past boogies with the future to bestow a joyous present. Since life is constant change, there's always something novel to experience and explore. Learning only needs to cease upon my last exhale.

Freedom lawyer hasn't lost a whit of his commitment, only changed his venue. He's expanded trial and error from the law to life itself— and hopes he still can learn from his mistakes.

WARRIOR'S EPILOGUE

My Favorite Polo Shot

Only in tournaments do I free my warrior.
"I'll do whatever it takes," it warns.
"That's why I brought you," I say.

Time's running out, our side is behind.
Suddenly teammate Susan breaks away,
streaks toward the goalposts with the ball.

I cover her six and ride off a rival
as she blasts her shot towards goal.
It slices wide to the right!

"Go, Zarahas!" warrior yells,
and my Arab leaps at the ball,
instantly accelerating to top speed.

We reach it ten yards before
it would sail out of bounds,
but we're too far to its right!

Warrior leans way out, grunts,
and whips a desperate forehand
across and under Raa's neck.

We plunge out of bounds, seeing
just a blur of white heading
for a foot-wide gap between
the goalposts at this slant.

Regaining balance, reining in
Zarahas, we hear the crowd roar:
Warrior scored.

AUTHOR BIOGRAPHY

Art Campbell was born in Brooklyn, raised in Appalachia, and scholarshipped to Harvard and Georgetown Universities. Prior to earning his second law degree he was a road-maintenance worker, janitor, boxer, rugby player, and professional musician. He became a trial lawyer for and against the government in Washington, D.C., where he also supervised students in the D.C. Law Students In Court program.

Campbell later moved to San Diego, became a tenured professor at California Western School of Law, and authored the country's definitive treatise on criminal sentencing. Married to the best-selling novelist Drusilla Campbell, they raised two sons and now enjoy training large dogs and horses.

CPSIA information can be obtained
at www.ICGtesting.com
Printed in the USA
FSOW04n1312120615
7881FS

9 780985 288334